Marry Me!

Marry Me!

Courtships and Proposals

of Legendary Couples

Wendy Goldberg and Betty Goodwin

♦

A Fireside Book
Published by Simon & Schuster
New York   London   Toronto
Sydney   Tokyo   Singapore

FIRESIDE
Rockefeller Center
1230 Avenue of the Americas
New York, NY 10020

First Fireside Edition 1996
Published by arrangement with Angel City Press

FIRESIDE and colophon are registered trademarks
of Simon & Schuster Inc.

Designed by Maureen Erbe and Rita A. Sowins

Manufactured in the United States of America

1   3   5   7   9   10   8   6   4   2

Library of Congress Cataloging-in-Publication Data
Goldberg, Wendy (date)
Marry me! : courtships and proposals of legendary couples /
Wendy Goldberg and Betty Goodwin. — 1st Fireside ed.
        p.   cm.
Includes bibliographical references (p.   ).
1. Courtship—History.   2. Marriage proposals—History.
I. Goodwin, Betty.   II. Title.
HQ801.G583   1996
306.73'4'09—dc20   95-25276
CIP
ISBN 0-684-81597-4

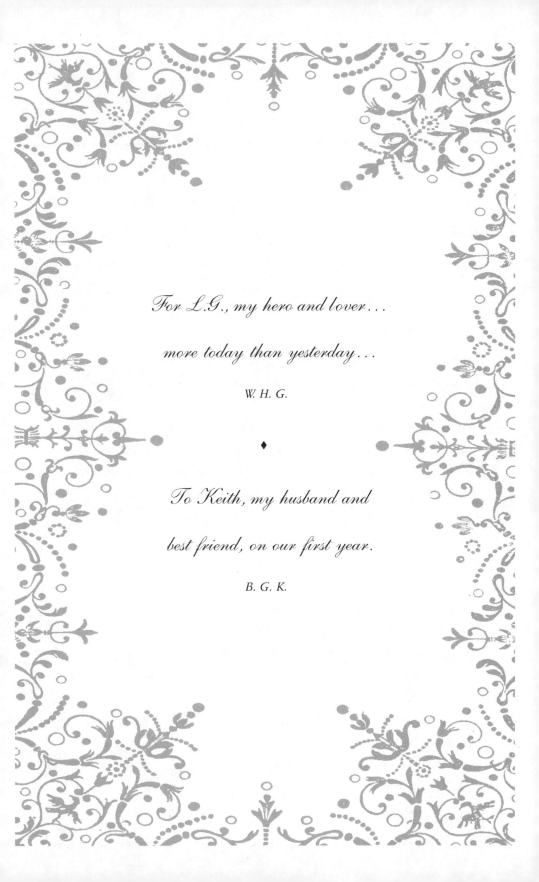

For L.G., my hero and lover…

more today than yesterday…

W. H. G.

♦

To Keith, my husband and

best friend, on our first year.

B. G. K.

Table of Contents

Table of Contents

Introduction

"**M**arry me!" *Two words that change your life.*
Why do we care to look back on a century of celebrated trips to the altar? Because romance is a part of all of our lives. Because glimpsing into the private worlds of famous people reveals that their pursuit of love is often no different than it is for the rest of us. (In fact, many of the couples tied the knot long before they became legends.) And because the instant when two people decide to marry is probably the most important and intimate moment of their lives – the peak of romance.

Yet, when the passions of public figures are played out on a public stage, society can play a role in their love stories too. Ultimately, King Edward VIII of England bowed to the demands of his country and renounced his throne rather than give up the woman he loved. Carlo Ponti was charged with bigamy and Sophia Loren branded a *"concubina"* when the Catholic Church chose not to recognize the film producer's Mexican divorce and the couple's subsequent Mexican marriage. Movie mogul Louis B. Mayer so feared any hint of scandal associated with his costly epic *Gone With the Wind* that he made a financial arrangement with its star, Clark Gable, enabling him to divorce his wife and legalize his long-term partnership with Carole Lombard.

Many of the couples who opened up to us were hesitant at first. Indeed, three who initially agreed to be included, begged out – they wanted to keep their private lives private. (We complied.) For the rest, once they decided to talk, their stories flowed. Nancy Reagan grew teary during our meeting as she remembered cherished words from her Ronnie. Dale Evans lovingly hand-wrote her recollections of the earliest days with Roy Rogers. For all, the details of their treasured love stories were as fresh in their minds as if it all happened yesterday.

There was a common tone in their voices and in their letters – triumph. The details change, the social circumstances vary, but marriage frequently occurs against all odds.

For many the decision to marry took contemplation and soul searching. Coretta Scott turned to prayer for guidance at the crucial juncture in her romance with Dr. Martin Luther King, Jr. And even for Janet Jones and Wayne Gretzky, whose romance seemed fast and easy, six years passed between their first meeting and their first date.

As for decision-making, several statesmen, or future statesmen, fell into the impulsive category. Prince Rainier III had virtually just met Grace Kelly when he asked for her hand. Lyndon Johnson popped the question to Lady Bird Taylor on their first date. Anwar Sadat and Jehan Safwat Raouf were acquainted for less than a month when they made engagement plans. Dr. King didn't come right out and ask, but he made his intentions clear to Coretta before he took her home after their first date.

It is fitting to begin this book with the romance of Dr. Sigmund Freud. After all, think of the many hours troubled lovers have spent on the couch thanks to him.

In the one hundred twelve years since Dr. Freud first became besotted with Martha Bernays, the impulse to mate remains unchanged, though methods of courtship have undeniably transformed. In Dr. Freud's day, personal encounters were often limited, therefore amorous communication frequently depended on the written word. For history's sake, such love notes are gold ore – it means that the renowned doctor's actual letter of proposal can be reprinted here. While the telephone improved contact between distant couples, it virtually destroyed the definitive evidence of romantic words and feelings. Lovers' memories are often all we can rely on.

The nature of proposals themselves isn't always what the fairy tales lead us to believe. Getting down on bended knee must be something that happens more in movies than in real life. Only two future husbands – Elvis Presley and Al Joyner – fell to their knees to do their asking. In Joyner's case, he knelt inside a limousine. For that matter, cars unquestionably proved to be a conducive setting. Neil Simon, Michael Caine, Ozzie Nelson and Michael Douglas all proposed in automobiles.

As for the magic words in the stories recounted in this book, men did all the asking (at least when someone actually asked). But, that's not to say that women didn't engage in their share of discussion, orchestration or negotiation before the finale.

Compiling a compelling list of couples meant looking at people who were universally fascinating. Even though some of the marriages ended in divorce – Marilyn Monroe and Joe DiMaggio were husband and wife for only nine months; Lucille Ball's union with second husband Gary Morton endured considerably longer than her fabled marriage to Desi Arnaz; and Priscilla Beaulieu and Elvis Presley separated after just six years of marriage – they were pairs that seemed linked for eternity in the public's mind. We decided to leave out legends with multiple famous spouses – choosing *which* of their courtships to record proved too daunting.

Finally, it took two gushy romantics to write a book of this nature – one was lovingly united in a twenty-one-year marriage; the other was impatiently waiting for hers to begin (and it did, just weeks before this book was completed).

My most brilliant achievement was my ability to persuade my wife to marry me. — Winston Churchill

Martha Bernays and Sigmund Freud

Married September 13, 1886

It was love at first sight for the father of psychoanalysis. Years after his marriage to Martha Bernays, Sigmund Freud told a friend that small decisions should be carefully weighed. However, he went on, life's critical issues, such as the selection of a spouse, should come from the unconscious mind. That's how it happened when the twenty-six-year-old struggling Viennese scientist met a petite, well-to-do brunette in his family's parlor and became instantly infatuated.

It was April 1882. A year after earning his medical degree, Sigmund, son of Jakob and Amalie Freud, was still living at home. His father, a wool and textile manufacturer struggling to keep his business together, had two sons from a previous marriage. He was forty when he married Amalie, and they had five daughters and three sons.

Sigmund was good-looking, with dark eyes, but his romantic life was wanting. He reportedly had few sexual experiences. No women had appealed to him since he was sixteen and fell in love with a childhood friend to whom he was too timid to speak. The brilliant young man never stopped to flirt with his sisters' friends. Instead, he'd go straight to his room to study. At the time, he wasn't interested in being a physician. Instead, he worked and taught in the zoological and anatomical laboratories of Ernst Brücke.

Martha, twenty-one, had her pick of admirers and had already rejected one prospective husband. She was confident and strong-willed, though sweet-natured, and came from a distinguished German Orthodox Jewish family who had moved from Hamburg to Vienna in 1869 when she was a child. Her late father, Berman, had been a merchant and her grandfather, Isaac, was Chief Rabbi of Hamburg.

On this particular evening, however, when he arrived home from the laboratory, he was immediately beguiled. On strictly aesthetic terms, Sigmund didn't agree with the many people who considered Martha a beauty. Sigmund said he considered physical perfection fleeting anyway and claimed he was attracted by Martha's entire being.

He showed her no evidence of interest for several weeks. Then suddenly, he decided to make his feelings known. Every day he sent Martha a single red rose, always accompanied with his visiting card on which he scrawled a note, written in either Latin, Spanish, English or German. He referred to her as "my Princess."

By the end of May, the couple was alone together for the first time. As they walked together, Sigmund offered Martha a bunch of oak leaves. She turned them down. The next day, they walked with her mother and Martha was confused by Sigmund's many questions and insatiable curiosity about her.

In early June, when the couple was strolling in a garden, they came across a double almond, or *Vielliebchen*, which signified that they were required to give each other a gift. Sigmund sent Martha a copy of the book *David Copperfield*. For her part, Martha baked a cake and accompanied it with a gracious note thanking Sigmund for the book.

On June 13, when Martha came to dinner at the Freuds', Sigmund seized her calling card. The flattered Martha touched his hand under the table, a display of affection that Sigmund's sisters couldn't help but observe. A day later, Martha wrote Sigmund a note. There was another walk. Another gift – a lime blossom from Martha to Sigmund.

On June 15, Sigmund wrote Martha an impassioned letter asking permission to address her using the informal, familiar German you, or *du*, the pronoun used for addressing children, lovers or those with whom one was on intimate terms. In late-nineteenth-century Victorian society, it was not only a decisive gesture, but Sigmund's manner of proposing marriage.

My sweet darling girl, … I cannot say here to Martha what I still have to say. I lack the confidence to finish the sentence, the line that the girl's glance and gesture forbids or allows. I will only allow myself to say one thing: the last time that we see each other I should like to address the loved one, the adored one, as 'Du,' and be assured of a relationship which perhaps will have for long to be veiled in secrecy.

How much I venture in writing that! If Martha's mood does not respond to mine when she reads these lines released from all restraint she will laugh at me or withdraw in annoyance. And I have to wait a long and fateful day until I read in her eyes the dispersal of my fears.

But I venture, and I am not writing to a stranger, but to the girl whom I may call my dearest friend – it is true, only since a few days, but nevertheless through countless threads of thought.

For the friend's consideration of this letter begs her
Dr. Sigmund Freud

Two days later, Martha responded by giving Sigmund a pearl ring that had belonged to her late father. They kept the engagement secret, perhaps because Sigmund didn't have the means to marry a rich Hamburg girl. First he had to earn enough money to support her in the manner in which she was accustomed. He made a copy of the ring for Martha and gave it to her to maintain the deception. Sigmund wasn't able to afford to buy Martha a proper engagement ring – set with a garnet – until a year and a half later.

To keep their betrothal to themselves, they concealed their letters to each other. Martha addressed hers to the laboratory, while those from Sigmund were sent in envelopes pre-addressed in a male friend's handwriting.

Could it be love that launched psychoanalysis? It was at this time that Sigmund made a monumental decision to become a physician. In order to start his own practice, however, he needed experience with patients. At the end of July, he began three years of intensive training at *Allgemeine Krankenhaus*, the main hospital of Vienna.

Six months after Martha and Sigmund were secretly engaged, Martha's brother Eli became engaged to Sigmund's oldest sister, Anna. Now, Martha and Sigmund felt it was safe to share their own happy news.

A year following the engagement, the couple faced a major setback when Martha's mother, Emmeline, decided to move her family back to Wandsbek, a suburb of Hamburg.

Freud was in no position to stop Martha, but he resented her devotion to her mother. He disapproved of her yielding to Emmeline's unilateral decision to leave Vienna, as well as the way Martha observed her mother's rigid Orthodox rituals.

After the move, they rarely saw each other. Freud was also intensely jealous, forbidding Martha to go ice skating for fear that she would hold hands with a man. His angry rebukes about Martha's acquiescing to her mother, as well as his jealousies of other men she might encounter, were outlined and referred to in some of the lengthy and copious love letters they exchanged. Sigmund's alone – scrawled in Gothic characters, at Martha's request – accounted for some nine hundred. The epistles became part of their private "Chronicle," which they planned to destroy upon their marriage. In his letters, Sigmund not only talked of romance but of his work, friends and associates.

After receiving a grant to study neuropathology in Paris, Sigmund finally opened his own neuropathology practice in April 1886 in Vienna. He was intent on finding a way to marry Martha now. Engagements of ten or fifteen years were not out of the question in their society, but Sigmund found the thought unbearable.

Money was still his biggest problem. He was significantly in debt and borrowing even more money to live. He had hoped his research, such as his studies on the physiological and therapeutic effects of cocaine (which he ingested in small doses to ward off depression and indigestion), would make him famous and create an onslaught of patients.

To help out, a sympathetic rich aunt offered Martha a sizeable dowry. There was also Martha's inheritance, but it still wasn't enough to pay for Martha's trousseau, the wedding, honeymoon, furniture and rent, plus the funds Sigmund gave to his own family. Further complicating matters was Sigmund's draft notice for five or six weeks of army maneuvers, which would mean losing more than a month's fees. On the plus side, an aunt and uncle of Martha's sent money as a wedding present.

After a chaste engagement of four and a half years, Martha, twenty-five, and Sigmund, thirty, were finally married in a civil ceremony at Wandsbek's Town Hall on September 13, 1886. The following day, the couple was married in a Jewish ceremony at Emmeline's house. Sigmund, who considered himself Jewish but was non-practicing, objected to a religious service, but it was necessary since Austria didn't recognize civil marriages. Sigmund managed to buy Martha a gold watch as a wedding present. They honeymooned in Lübeck, Travemunde, Berlin, Dresden and Brunn.

The first month of marriage was happy, but business was abysmal. Sigmund pawned his gold watch to pay the rent and would have pawned Martha's as well were it not for a last-minute donation by her sister, Minna.

Since Sigmund was very fond of children, the Freuds had three sons and three daughters. Minna joined the household and lived with the family until her death. The Freuds' daughter Anna became one of her father's most renowned followers.

The most difficult clients are psychotherapists,
reveals a third-generation New York matchmaker. "They analyze everyone."

Zelda Sayre and F. Scott Fitzgerald

Married April 3, 1920

Afer they married at the dawn of the Jazz Age, F. Scott Fitzgerald and Zelda Sayre became superstars of the era, symbolizing "flaming youth," success and charming recklessness. For the nearly two years it took Scott to woo Zelda, the effect was alternately frustrating and motivating, and indisputably the source of inspiration for the novels and short stories that brought him success.

The engaging young man from St. Paul, Minnesota, was given the imposing name Francis Scott Key Fitzgerald (for his famous, distant relative) and was known to everyone as Scott. He grew up painfully self-conscious about his family's less than impressive social stature. His mother, Mollie, came from prosperous stock; his father, Edward, was unable to properly support the family.

With some of his mother's inheritance, the gifted boy was able to enter aristocratic Princeton University, where he spent most of his time writing for campus magazines and theater productions and eventually became the school's most famous dropout. In 1917, he joined the Army with heroic dreams of going overseas to fight in World War I.

At twenty-one, he was stationed in Camp Sheridan, near Montgomery, Alabama. In July 1918, he attended a dance at the Montgomery Country Club. There, dressed in his lieutenant's uniform tailored by Brooks Brothers and with his blond hair characteristically parted in the middle, he met Zelda, a belle who had just graduated from high school and whose eighteenth birthday was a week away.

A year and a half earlier, Scott had been bewitched by Ginevra King, a rich, beautiful and popular high-society girl with whom a future together was unlikely.

Zelda wasn't rich – her father was Alabama Supreme Court Judge Anthony Sayre – but her reputation as a coquette and heartbreaker had already spread throughout the state, and into Georgia as well. The golden-haired beauty was effervescent and carefree – she smoked, drank and did her utmost to live beyond the limits of southern propriety. She was the kind who blithely dropped her swimsuit and dove into a pool.

Zelda and Scott dazzled each other with their charms, he with his intelligence, dogged romancing and yearning for fame, she with her natural self-assurance and zest. Both craved glamour, excitement and money.

Whenever Scott could, he'd take the bus into Montgomery and, from the bus stop, ride a taxi to the Sayres' house at 6 Pleasant Avenue. If he couldn't visit, he phoned daily, sometimes twice. Zelda had more than her share of beaux, and Scott became just one of them. That summer, they sipped cool drinks, took long walks in the woods and swung on the Sayres' front porch. Scott carved their names in the doorpost of the country club.

Still, Zelda refused to drop her other admirers. Scott might be called off to war any time. And besides, he didn't have a dime to his name and she couldn't be certain of his prospects. Furthermore, her father disapproved of Scott's drinking.

By early fall, Scott, no less encouraged, noted in his ledger that he had fallen in love. In November, Scott's unit was sent to Camp Mills on Long Island to await embarkation, but the war ended before they were sent to France. He returned to Camp Sheridan to await his discharge, and renewed his intoxicating, though still uncertain, courtship.

By December, Zelda cared enough to invite him to her family's Christmas dinner, but afterwards she still saw other men, although Scott threw jealous fits that ended in drinking sprees. At one of the grandest balls of the year, in January, Zelda's dance card was too full for even a twirl with Scott.

In February, after his discharge from the Army, Scott left for New York, fully aware that Zelda wasn't going to commit until he was a "money-maker," as he wrote in his ledger. But his prospects were bleak. He was turned down for reporting jobs by seven newspapers and wound up taking a position writing slogans for an advertising company. He knew this wasn't going to get him anywhere with Zelda.

By night, he worked on his own writing, but over the course of three months received one hundred twenty-two rejection slips for his short stories. The couple exchanged amorous letters, Zelda dashing off her buoyant missives with idiosyncratic punctuation. (Only Scott's telegrams survive.) Zelda made frequent mention of marriage and her desire to put an end to her loneliness. Regardless, she kept a date with another flame, Auburn University football-hero Francis Stubbs.

In March, after receiving one particularly impassioned letter from Zelda, Scott arranged to give her an engagement ring which belonged to his mother. He wrote a letter asking Judge Sayre for his daughter's hand and sent Zelda a wire: "*Darling… the ring arrived tonight and I am sending it Monday. I love you and I thought I would tell you how much on this Saturday night when we ought to be together. Don't let your family be shocked at my present.*"

The ring arrived accompanied by Scott's calling card, on which he penned, *"Darling – I am sending this just the way it came – I hope it fits and I wish I were there to put it on. I love you so much, much, much that it just hurts every minute I'm without you – Do write every day because I love your letters so – Goodbye, My own Wife."*

When Zelda received the ring, she wrote back: *"Every time I see it on my finger I am rather startled – I've never worn a ring before, they've always seemed so inappropriate – but I love to see this shining there so nice and white like our love – And it sorter {sic} says 'Soon' to me all the time – Just sings it all day long."*

Still not thrilled about Scott's prospects as husband material, Zelda's parents didn't consider this an official engagement. Zelda continued to see local college boys, assuring Scott all the while in her letters that her escorts meant nothing.

Hardly consoled, Scott made three successive visits to Montgomery in the spring to keep the romance on track. Meanwhile, at the country club, Zelda met Perry Adair, a golfer from Georgia Tech. Soon she was off to Atlanta to attend Perry's commencement and a round of parties. At the train station, no less than four boys greeted her. By the time she came home, she and Perry were pinned. When Zelda had a change of mind and returned the boy's fraternity pin with a note, she inadvertently (or was it?) sent the letter to a newly enraged Scott.

He left for Montgomery, ordering that she marry him at once, but Zelda turned him down and gave back his engagement ring in June.

Depressed with his career and his love life, Scott quit his job and returned to St. Paul to rewrite a novel Scribner had twice rejected. In September, as soon as he finished *This Side of Paradise*, it was immediately accepted. Scott pleaded with his editor, Maxwell Perkins, to publish it quickly so that he could take the money to wed Zelda. No such luck. The book wouldn't be published until the following spring. Scott set out revising some of his rejected short stories and quickly sold fifteen of them to several magazines including *The Saturday Evening Post*. He returned to Montgomery to put their relationship back together.

By January, Scott was a literary darling and with his earnings he bought Zelda a diamond and platinum watch, inscribed "from Scott to Zelda." Zelda agreed to marry him when the first copies of his novel came off the presses.

This Side of Paradise, by F. Scott Fitzgerald, was published on March 26 and became an overnight hit. Advertisements for the book read, "A Novel About Flappers Written for Philosophers." On March 28, the couple's engagement appeared in the *Montgomery Journal*.

Zelda wrote Scott shortly before the wedding: *"Darling Heart, our fairy tale is almost ended, and we're going to marry and live happily every afterward just like the princess in her tower who worried you so much – and made me so very cross by her constant recurrence – I'm so sorry for all the times I've been mean and hateful – for all the miserable minutes I've caused you when we could have been so happy."*

The wedding was scheduled for April 5, but Scott couldn't wait for Zelda any longer. At the last minute he pushed the date up two days. Before noon on April 3, 1920, Scott, a Catholic, and Zelda, an Episcopalian, were married in the rectory of St. Patrick's Cathedral in New York. Zelda wore a deep blue suit and matching hat and clutched a bouquet of orchids. None of the couple's parents attended. Zelda's sister Rosalind Smith was matron of honor, and Ludlow Fowler, one of Scott's friends from Princeton, was best man. There was no reception.

For their honeymoon, the Fitzgeralds stayed at The Biltmore Hotel in New York until they were thrown out for creating disturbances. When the newlyweds moved over to the Commodore Hotel, they reportedly spun around the hotel's revolving door for a half hour. A daughter, Frances Scott (known as Scottie), was born one and a half years later.

"By all means marry; if you get a good wife, you'll become happy; if you get a bad one, you'll become a philosopher." – Socrates

Frida Kahlo and Diego Rivera

Married August 21, 1929

Diego Rivera, one of the greatest artists of the twentieth century, had four wives. But his third, the fascinating Frida Kahlo, an artist in her own right, was the focus of his most passionate and haunting affair.

Their lives initially intersected in 1922, when Diego, already a celebrated artist at thirty-six, painted his first mural in Mexico City in the amphitheater of the National Preparatory School. Born in Guanajuato, Mexico, Diego had studied painting in Spain and had settled in Paris for a decade, where he was a member of the avant-garde. In 1921, he had left behind his common-law wife, returned to his homeland and joined the Communist party. A lifelong revolutionary, he expressed his social and political convictions in monumental paintings that spoke to his countrymen. Brilliant, charismatic and a devoted lover of women, he often found those affections returned, even though he was overweight and incontestably ugly, with fuzzy hair and bulging eyes.

Frida was a student at the Preparatory who watched the famous artist with interest. She was bright and a definite tomboy who ran around with troublemakers. Petite and striking, her looks stemmed in part from her heritage: part German Jewish, part Spanish, part Indian. Her black eyebrows met over her nose and her right leg was withered from polio.

She was only fifteen, but she knew what she wanted.

"My ambition is to have a child by Diego Rivera," Frida immediately notified a friend. "And I'm going to tell him so someday."

To get the artist's attention, she mercilessly taunted him, calling him names like "Old Fatso" and playing pranks on him. On one occasion, she soaped the stairway Diego used every day, hoping that she could witness the national celebrity slip and fall, though he never did.

She tried hard to insult one of his models, Guadalupe Marin, a great beauty, whom he was then courting. But in due time, Guadalupe became Diego's second wife and the mother of two of his daughters. Frida, meanwhile, was the victim of a devastating streetcar accident in which her spine, collarbone, pelvis and right leg were broken and her right foot was crushed. She was confined to a plaster body cast for months. With her still-whole arms, she requested paint and canvas and began to hone the skills she would use to paint haunting and surreal self-portraits that mirrored her suffering and psyche.

Several years passed, and when Frida regained her mobility, though never full health, she tracked down Diego at the Ministry of Education, where he was working on another mural. She boldly asked the master to come down from his scaffolding to speak to her and critique the painting she had brought to show him. She wanted to know if he thought she could earn a living as an artist. Diego liked her work and wanted to see more, so she invited him to her family's house in Coyoacan, a suburb of Mexico City.

The two were to become soul mates on many levels.

Now divorced from Guadalupe, Diego was attracted to Frida, who had developed a political conscience of her own as a member of the Young Communist League. A few days after his visit, Diego kissed her for the first time. After he completed his work on the education building, he began to seriously court the young girl. Diego had many women in his life, but Frida matched wits with him and they could discuss everything. Soon he was asking her to critique *his* work, even though her opinions were sometimes brutal.

More than just intellectual equals, Frida and Diego were also aware of the palpable chemistry between them. Once when they were walking through Coyoacan, the street lights suddenly turned on. When Diego impulsively decided to kiss Frida, the light closest to them went out, and then went back on when they finished. They tested this phenomenon on other street lamps and witnessed the same results.

All of this electricity did not go unnoticed. After observing the lovers silently for a time, Frida's father, Guillermo Kahlo, felt duty bound to speak out.

"I see you are interested in my daughter, eh?"

"Yes," replied the artist. "Otherwise I would not come all the way out here to see her."

"Well, sir, I want to give you a warning. Frida is a clever girl, but she is *un demonio oculto* – a concealed devil. *Un demonio oculto!*"

"I know it," said Diego.

"Well, I have done my duty," sighed her father.

With that semi-blessing, Diego, forty-two, and Frida, twenty-two, were married on August 21, 1929. The civil ceremony in Coyoacan's city hall was attended only by Frida's father and three witnesses. Frida wore a Tehuana Indian costume that pleased Diego – a layered skirt, which concealed her bad foot, a blouse, shawl and beads. Diego dressed "American-style," in a suit without a vest. Afterwards, a few relatives and friends attended a celebration in their honor.

She never did have a child. With Diego she suffered one miscarriage and also had to have an abortion due to the position of the fetus.

Diego's work and fame spread throughout the world, and he resumed his lifelong habit of extramarital love affairs. It was easy for Frida, who kept her maiden name, to look the other way most of the time, since the couple lived in separate but adjoining houses. But she too began to have affairs – both with men, including Leon Trotsky, who had a house nearby, and with women. The couple began divorce proceedings in 1939.

Diego's profound love for Frida never died. After a year apart, while he was painting in San Francisco, he asked her to join him, on the pretext of consulting an important bone surgeon about her slowly deteriorating body. They remarried in a civil ceremony in San Francisco on December 8, 1940, Diego's fifty-fourth birthday. They stayed together until she died in 1954 at forty-seven.

Claudia "Lady Bird" Taylor and Lyndon Baines Johnson

Married November 17, 1934

Twenty-nine years before he was sworn in as the thirty-sixth president of the United States, Lyndon Baines Johnson launched a relentless campaign to win the hand of Claudia Taylor, a fellow Texan with the unusual nickname "Lady Bird."

Lyndon, who grew up a poor, small-town boy from a politically active Texas family, was an up and comer in the infancy of his political career. During a business trip to Austin, he had a date planned with another woman when he ran into his friend Eugenia Boehringer, who was with Lady Bird. Eugenia had previously talked about introducing him to Lady Bird, and he found himself immediately attracted to the sheltered and reserved young woman. Then serving his third year as secretary to a U.S. congressman from Texas, Lyndon had been elected speaker of the Little Congress in Washington, D.C., a sort of junior congress that had been established by congressional secretaries many years before. To everyone, including Lady Bird, this twenty-six-year-old man exuded unusual confidence and determination.

She was the daughter of the former Minnie Pattillo and her husband Thomas Jefferson Taylor, a wealthy Texas farmer and owner of general stores. Ambitious in her own way, Lady Bird had recently graduated from the University of Texas at Austin and went on to earn a second degree in journalism. She had also studied shorthand and typing, as many practical young women did at the time.

When she met Lyndon in the fall of 1934, she was twenty-one years old and still living in Karnack, Texas, with her widowed father. She had never had a serious boyfriend, yet she found herself strangely drawn to the tall, handsome and accomplished young man who pursued her with such vigor and determination.

That evening, Lyndon invited Lady Bird and Eugenia to join him and his date for drinks. The next day, he invited "Bird," as he called her, for breakfast, followed by a long drive in the country. She hedged about showing up and arrived late. But by day's end, Lyndon had proposed marriage.

She didn't say yes; she didn't say no. The young congressional aide returned to Washington without an answer. Over the next few weeks, while the couple corresponded and talked on the telephone, Lady Bird told him she thought it would be best if they waited a year before making a decision.

Ten weeks later, Lyndon returned to Texas and made it clear he wasn't going to be put off one moment longer. While Lady Bird refused to be pinned down to a wedding date, she told him she would accept an engagement ring. At home, she was getting conflicting advice. Her maiden aunt, who helped to raise her, advised caution. But her father approved of Lyndon. "Some of the best deals are made in a hurry," he told her.

The next day, on November 17, Lyndon gave Lady Bird an ultimatum. "We either do it now, or we never will," he said. "And if you say good-bye to me, it just proves to me that you don't love me enough to dare to. And I just can't bear to go and keep on wondering if it will ever happen."

She agreed to "do it now." That same day, they got in Lyndon's Ford and drove to San Antonio, where Lyndon knew the city postmaster, who secured the marriage license and arranged for a minister to marry them on short notice. The postmaster even brought over a dozen, $2.50 wedding bands from Sears, Roebuck, from which Lady Bird selected her size – and which the postmaster offered the couple as his wedding gift. Later, the couple picked out a ring with a small diamond flanked on both sides by three diamond baguettes.

That evening, Lyndon and Lady Bird were married at St. Mark's Episcopal Church. A supper at St. Anthony's Hotel followed. The Johnsons spent their wedding night at the Plaza Hotel in San Antonio, and set off the very next day in the Ford for Mexico. They stopped in Monterrey, San Luis Potosi and Mexico City, climbing every pyramid along the way.

After three miscarriages which caused the couple tremendous sorrow, their daughter, Lynda Bird, was born in 1944, followed by another girl, Lucy Baines, in 1947.

*The engagement and wedding rings
are placed on the third finger of the left hand because of the romantic
notion that its vein extends directly to the heart.*

Harriet Hilliard and Ozzie Nelson

Married October 8, 1935

Ozzie Nelson's adventures with Harriet Hilliard really began in 1932 when he caught the shapely blonde's singing act at the Hollywood Restaurant, then one of the most popular nightclubs in Manhattan. He was looking to spruce up his band, Ozzie Nelson and His Orchestra, and Harriet, a twenty-year-old, fresh-faced beauty seemed just the ticket. He quickly suggested that she sing "boy-girl" duets with him.

The twenty-six-year-old from Jersey City, New Jersey, was kind of cute, Harriet remembers. And the former football star from Rutgers University was already making a name for himself on the college-band circuit.

But Harriet was a seasoned vaudeville performer and was earning more money than Ozzie could pay her. She thought twice about accepting his offer and sought counsel from a friend.

"Why don't you try it for the summer, Harriet? I think he's going to go far, and I'd like to see you hitch your wagon to that star," Harriet recalls her friend advising her.

Ozzie and Harriet toured together for the next two years, but their romance took a long time in developing. At first, they were both distracted by other admirers. They gradually learned, however, that they had an amazing amount in common.

Both had started their careers at an early age, were hard-working and, in the midst of the Depression, had personal financial constraints. Harriet was supporting her mother, and Ozzie, while simultaneously attending law school and working as a high-school coach, was helping to put his younger brother through school. They both also came from modest show-business families.

Before they were married, Ozzie's parents were an amateur minstrel show act known as Nelson and Orr. While George Nelson continued to earn a living as a bank clerk, he recruited his middle son, five-year-old Ozzie, for the act. By high school,

Ozzie had formed his first band.

Harriet's parents, Roy Hilliard and Hazel McNutt, were both well-known stock actors, and Harriet made her first stage appearance at the age of six weeks. At fifteen, she left Des Moines for New York to study ballet and work in vaudeville.

In the summer of 1935, as the band became more successful, it seemed inevitable that Ozzie would ask Harriet to marry him. The first few times she refused. She wasn't ready, she told him. But it didn't take her long to change her mind.

One day in August while they were driving from a ballroom booking in Henderson, Texas, to an appearance at the Cocoanut Grove in Los Angeles, she was hoping he'd pop the question again.

Harriet turned to Ozzie and said, "You haven't said anything for the past fifty miles. Are you still with us?"

"Yeah," he said. "I've been thinking about us. I think we've got enough money saved up now so we can get married. What do you think?"

"Sounds good to me. In fact, I thought you'd never ask."

Ozzie couldn't afford to buy a diamond engagement ring. But Harriet received a gold band when they were married on October 8, 1935, at his mother's apartment in Hacksensack, New Jersey. They were surrounded by family members and a phalanx of reporters. For several years, Ozzie performed in radio and in ballrooms while Harriet was making movies. But on their ninth anniversary, the couple reunited for a radio show called *The Adventures of Ozzie & Harriet,* with actors standing in for their young sons David and Ricky. After making two movies together, the entire Nelson family went before television cameras to portray themselves in the popular series of the same name from 1952 to 1966. As the fans of that show might remember, many were the times Harriet would gently throw Ozzie a line and then quip, as he went for the bait, "Gee Ozzie, I thought you'd never ask."

"Love does not consist in gazing at each other,
but in looking outward together in the same direction."
— Antoine de Saint-Exupéry

Wallis Simpson and
His Majesty King Edward VIII of England

Married June 3, 1937

The so-called love affair of the century – in which a king gave up his throne for the woman he loved – was kismet, or so it appears.

When she was going through her first divorce, Wallis Warfield Spencer was told by an astrologer she would marry two more times, undergo several serious emotional crises and, between the ages of forty and fifty, become an extremely powerful woman through a relationship with an influential man. At about the same time, Edward Albert Christian George Andrew Patrick David, the Prince of Wales and future King of England, also reportedly consulted an astrologer, who predicted that he would fall deeply in love with a woman for whom he would relinquish everything.

All of these predictions came to pass in what was to become the most famous love story of the twentieth century. Wallis divorced her first husband, a navy aviator, Earl Winfield Spencer, Jr., in 1927 after an eleven-year marriage. A year later, in 1928, she married Ernest Simpson, a half-English, half-American Harvard dropout who was also divorced. In the midst of the Depression, Ernest and Wallis moved to London where he worked for a ship brokerage. They settled into a flat that Wallis promptly set about decorating, employing four full-time servants and one part-time servant.

Wallis' first brush with royalty actually occurred in April 1920. There was a reception in the prince's honor on the *U.S.S. New Mexico* in San Diego, California. Lieutenant Spencer and his young wife attended – but they did not attend the ball that evening at the Hotel del Coronado, where lore has it that the future lovers first laid eyes on each other.

Wallis and David, as the prince was known to intimates, met again in 1930 or 1931 – recollections differ – at a party given by Lady Thelma Furness. After the festivities, the prince offered the Simpsons a lift home.

This was no ordinary lift. David was considered the most eligible bachelor on earth. Modest, handsome and famously chic, he was a man of numerous pursuits: needlepoint, fox hunting, horseback riding, bagpipe playing, golf, gardening – and getting involved with married, and therefore always unavailable, women such as Thelma, another American.

In January 1932, David invited the Simpsons to spend a weekend at his country home, Fort Belvedere, and many more weekends followed. On such occasions, there were usually about three other couples in attendance, plus Thelma, who had been seeing David since 1929. She and Wallis became friends.

Later that year, on June 19, David, possibly at Thelma's urging, gathered some friends for a dinner party in London at Quaglino's in honor of Wallis' thirty-sixth birthday. He gave Wallis an orchid plant, informing her that if cared for properly, it would bloom again in a year.

One year later, Wallis couldn't help but see the symbolism of the flowering orchid. It was at this time that Thelma had to depart for the United States, where her twin sister, Gloria Vanderbilt, was involved with a custody suit over her ten-year-old daughter, also named Gloria. Before leaving, Thelma lunched with Wallis at the Ritz and asked her to "look after" David while she was gone. While Thelma was away, the prince began regularly dropping in unannounced for dinner at the Simpsons', enjoying more than the fried chicken, soups and stews that came out of the kitchen that Wallis expertly supervised.

Though few considered Wallis a beauty, she was slim, extremely fashionable and had dazzling blue eyes. Cecil Beaton, who would photograph her often, found her "attractively ugly." More important, she was clever, alluring and a good talker who peppered her conversations with Americanisms that tickled the prince. She was also an able listener who took great interest in David's "princing" rounds, no matter how dull. By the time Thelma returned a few months later, she had been replaced.

In 1934, the year David turned forty, he and Wallis shared a summer interlude alone, or at least without Ernest. David had rented a house in Biarritz and invited Wallis and Ernest to be his guests, but Ernest had to be in New York on business. Wallis went anyway, with her Aunt Bessie Merryman acting as chaperone. Minus Aunt Bessie, the couple, plus assorted friends and aides cruised the Mediterranean. Wallis and David occasionally slipped off to a bistro for a private dinner. In Cannes, David bought Wallis a diamond-and-emerald charm for her bracelet. It is believed that David decided he would marry Wallis that year. He somehow believed that he had the power and right to marry any woman he wanted.

In spite of the astrologer's prophecy, Wallis, frankly, saw her relationship with David as one of life's supreme larks and never imagined it would last forever. By 1935, though she was still very much in David's life, he was also occupied with the Silver Jubilee of his father, King George V, and the marriage of his brother, Prince Henry. Then on January 20, 1936, the king died, and David acceded to the throne. Some of those around him believed he was less interested in his duties than he was in Wallis.

A six-month period of mourning followed, during which the prince could not see Wallis in public. Still, they attended private parties together. Around this time, David also asked Ernest to allow Wallis to divorce him.

In May, David decided it was time to be more open about his relationship and told Wallis, "It's got to be done. Sooner or later my prime minister must meet my future wife."

Wallis had never heard him verbalize his intentions until that moment, and it suddenly frightened her.

"David," she protested, "you mustn't talk that way. The idea is impossible. They'd never let you."

"I'm well aware of that, but rest assured, I will manage it somehow."

On May 27, David invited Prime Minister Stanley Baldwin and his wife, Lucy, to dinner with Wallis and other guests, including Ernest. Wallis' leading role in David's life was obvious to everyone.

In August, the couple took a very public, month-long Greek and Turkish cruise, meeting heads of state and royalty along the way. The affair was public now – except in England. While newspapers in Europe and the United States ran splashy stories about the king and his mistress, the British press agreed to keep mum.

Meanwhile, with Wallis' divorce action in progress, David formally proposed, planning to marry her in time for his coronation on May 12, 1937. The British press finally broke its silence about the woman in the king's life, and the romance suddenly became too hot to handle. With her picture emblazoned across all the British papers, Wallis fled to Cannes. When she left, David told her, "I don't know how it's all going to end. It will be some time before we can be together again. You must wait for me no matter how long it takes. I shall never give you up."

It is a fundamental principle of the British constitution that the monarch must accept the advice of the prime minister and the cabinet – the twenty or so leading members of Parliament who carry out executive functions. Baldwin now informed the king that the cabinet advised him not to marry Wallis, since it was clear that pubic opinion in the United Kingdom and in the Commonwealth was strongly opposed to it. David knew that if he acted against this advice, the cabinet would resign, there would be a constitutional crisis, and the future of the monarchy would consequently be endangered.

He felt he had no choice but to abdicate on December 11, 1936. He broadcast a farewell message in which he said he "found it impossible to carry the heavy burden of responsibility and to discharge my duties as King as I would wish to do without the help and support of the woman I love." He immediately departed for Vienna.

"The drawbridges are going up behind me," he told Wallis. "I have taken you into a void."

In March 1937, Wallis left for Tours, France, home of Charles Bedaux, who offered his chateau for the wedding. Divorce laws required the couple to stay apart until

Wallis' divorce was granted on April 27. At long last, David was able to join her in France. Wallis, who was supposedly superstitious about a May marriage ("Marry in May and rue the day," the saying goes), wanted to postpone the nuptials until June. For his part, David preferred to delay the event until after his brother Albert's coronation on May 12. They settled on June 3.

American couturier Mainbocher designed Wallis' trousseau, including her wedding gown of blue crepe satin with a short, fitted jacket. The shade of blue, said to match the decor of the chateau's salon, was dubbed "Wallis blue." The day before the nuptials, Cecil Beaton took formal photographs of the couple. That same day, David was informed by his brother, King George VI, that he had been given a new title, His Royal Highness, the Duke of Windsor, but Wallis would be known only as the Duchess of Windsor. Their children, he was also informed, could not inherit his title.

Just before noon, Wallis and David were married by the mayor of Monts, followed by a religious service. Aunt Bessie was among the sixteen guests. The king, queen, queen mother and Winston Churchill sent congratulatory telegrams.

Wallis wore a hat of tiny feathers trimmed with a tulle halo. On her right wrist was a wide diamond-and-sapphire bracelet, known as the "marriage contract" bracelet; she also wore a matching brooch and earrings. David's wedding present to her was a diamond bracelet with nine dangling Latin crosses set with gemstones. Her engagement ring was a 19.77 carat rectangular emerald from Cartier London. The stone was one half of one of the greatest emeralds in the world, once belonging to the Grand Mogul. The ring was inscribed, "We are ours now 27 x 36." The date, October 27, 1936, marked their engagement day. In the couple's private code, "we" represented the initials of their first names.

The couple honeymooned in Venice. They had no children.

The diamond engagement ring should be about fourteen percent of the total wedding expense, suggests Bridal Guide magazine, and other experts recommend spending two months' salary on this lasting symbol of love. The Guide also suggests budgeting one hundred dollars for a prenuptial agreement.

Carole Lombard and Clark Gable

Married March 29, 1939

Carole Lombard may have lost out in getting the role she coveted – Scarlett O'Hara – but she won Clark Gable's heart when he was starring as Rhett Butler in *Gone With the Wind* in 1939.

By then Gable and Lombard had been an "item" in the gossip columns for three years. The two sex symbols – both phenomenally popular with the public – met at the Mayfair Ball at Victor Hugo's restaurant in Beverly Hills in January 1936, the year after Clark won an Academy Award for *It Happened One Night* and Carole starred in several films, including *My Man Godfrey*. The fete was Hollywood's answer to swank affairs tossed by Los Angeles' upper crust society, who didn't invite Hollywood types. Carole and Clark, who had worked with each other on *No Man of Her Own* three years earlier, quarreled during the party. Three days later, Carole sent Clark, then living alone at the Beverly Wilshire Hotel, white doves as a peace offering.

The next month they ran into each other again at the "Nervous Breakdown" ball given by John Hay Whitney. Living up to her reputation as Hollywood's wackiest blonde, Carole staged an entrance via stretcher and ambulance. Clark was impressed, and Carole was taken by his rakish charm.

She was a girl who knew how to get what she wanted. Soon after, on St. Valentine's Day, Carole, aware of Clark's fondness for expensive cars, bought a dilapidated old jalopy, painted it white with red hearts and delivered it to Metro-Goldwyn-Mayer.

Soon after, they began seeing each other. Clark had his share of extramarital affairs, but he was enthralled with Carole, who never took his enormous fame too seriously. When Clark was crowned "The King of Hollywood" on NBC (the "Queen" was Myrna Loy), Carole had no reason to feel insecure – in 1937, she had been Hollywood's highest-paid actress.

A well-known prankster, nothing was sacred to "Ma," as Clark called her, not even

"Pa's" false teeth. ("Mammy" and "Pappy" were their other pet names.) She constantly reminded him of his notorious flop, *Parnell,* and once had leaflets printed and passed out at MGM extolling the film's one good review – in China. "Fifty Million Chinamen Can't Be Wrong!" read her message. Even their feuds were colorful. After arguments, Carole dispatched more caged birds, though she began to accuse Clark of eating them.

Their relationship was not without a taint of scandal. Carole was divorced from William Powell, but Clark was still married to Ria, a rich socialite seventeen years his senior, and there were no immediate plans for divorce. Notoriously frugal, Clark may have been stalling because he didn't want to part with the large financial settlement Ria demanded. This was a problem, not only for the lovers, but for Louis B. Mayer, whose MGM studios had Clark under contract – and that contract included a morality clause.

Though she was a renowned party girl, Carole dropped out of the social scene in favor of pursuing virile activities Clark enjoyed – watching boxing matches, baseball at Gilmore Field and horse racing at Santa Anita, as well as going fishing, skeet shooting and game hunting.

Clark wasn't interested in the part of Rhett Butler – his bad experience in period costume for *Parnell* was not forgotten – but he had no choice. Producer David O. Selznick wanted Clark, who was still under contract at MGM, and Carole strongly encouraged him to take it. Selznick went to Mayer, his father-in-law, to borrow Clark plus arrange for financing in exchange for distribution rights and fifty percent of the net proceeds for seven years. In addition to a large bonus, the studio sweetened the deal by offering Clark a financial incentive to assist him with his divorce.

At the same time, a shocking *Photoplay* magazine article entitled "Hollywood's Unmarried Husbands and Wives" named them, further prompting the couple to make their relationship legal. With so much on the line with *Gone With the Wind*, Mayer wasn't going to have the movie's star embroiled in disgrace, and saw to it that Clark put his love life in order. Clark agreed to give Ria a huge settlement and she officially filed for divorce. Once the divorce was granted on March 8, 1939, Carole told gossip columnist Louella Parsons, "When Clark gets a few days off, perhaps we'll sneak away and have the ceremony performed."

Sure enough, two months after filming began on *Gone With The Wind* and three weeks after Victor Fleming replaced George Cukor as director on the set, Clark took six days off. To escape the press, he told no one of their plans. On the morning of March 29, 1939, the couple left for Kingman, Arizona, driven the four hundred miles by MGM publicist Otto Winkler in his blue DeSoto coupe. Mrs. Winkler supplied sandwiches. Just outside of Los Angeles, they stopped at a florist shop, where Clark bought two carnation boutonnieres and a corsage of lilies of the valley and pink roses for Carole.

They arrived in Kingman that afternoon and went directly to the town hall for their marriage license. The couple changed into their wedding clothes at the home of Reverend Kenneth Engel. Carole wore a gray flannel suit with a black-and-white polka-dot vest fashioned by the costume designer Irene, who designed many of her film wardrobes. Clark wore a blue serge suit.

In the rectory of the First Methodist Episcopal Church, Mrs. Engel played "Here Comes the Bride" on the organ. Clark, thirty-eight, slipped a platinum band on the finger of his thirty-year-old bride. Before the newlyweds departed, they stopped at the local telegraph office to let David Selznick in on their secret by sending him a six-word message: *"Married this afternoon – Carole and Clark."*

Once past the state line, the wedding party stopped for a steak dinner at the Harvey House in Needles and then drove on to Carole's Bel-Air home. The next morning, they held court at a press conference arranged by MGM and catered by the Brown Derby, one of the couple's favorite restaurants. Carole told Louella that she planned to work for a few more years and then start a family. "I'll let Pa be the star and I'll stay home, darn socks and look after the kids."

On their first anniversary, Carole had Clark's dressing room done up with satin, tulle and flowers and created a nest in which she deposited a large egg with *Parnell* scrawled across it.

In January 1942, Carole joined the entertainment community's efforts to help finance the war. Returning from a successful bond-selling tour, Carole was killed in a plane crash, that also killed her mother, Bessie Peters, and their friend, Otto Winkler. A year later, the disconsolate Clark joined the Air Force, flying several bombing missions over Germany. He eventually remarried twice. Clark died on November 19, 1960, five months before his son, John Clark Gable, was born.

Lucille Ball and Desi Arnaz

Married November 30, 1940

Although Lucille Ball and Desi Arnaz seemed interchangeable with Lucy and Ricky Ricardo, their comic alter egos on the hit television series, *I Love Lucy,* roles were reversed when it came to a marriage plan. On the small screen, Lucy may have been the behind-the-scenes schemer, but in real life, eleven years before their historic TV run began, it was Desi who plotted behind Lucy's back to arrange a surprise wedding with less than twenty-four hours' notice.

They first became linked in 1940 at RKO as co-stars of the movie *Too Many Girls.* Desi, a twenty-three-year-old Cuban bandleader and bongo player who was a big hit in New York, was making his motion picture debut. Lucille (Desi was the only one who called her Lucy in those days), six years his senior, had already made about forty films. They were immediately attracted to each other and became a couple about town.

After filming was completed, Desi began touring and Lucy remained in Hollywood to make another picture. It was the first of many long separations. Both were intensely possessive, each one accusing the other of infidelities.

The love affair was on rocky ground when Lucy was in New York later that year to promote the film *Dance, Girl, Dance,* and Desi was in town appearing at the Roxy Theatre. During an interview in her suite at the Pierre Hotel, Lucy, who must have still been brooding over her latest tiff with Desi, spelled out to a woman reporter all the perfectly logical reasons why she would never marry Desi, starting with the most obvious: he was bound to the nightclub circuit and she was committed to Hollywood.

Desi, who was in the next room, heard the whole thing. He was waiting to sweep her off her feet, and he did so as soon as the interview was over. They kissed, made up and made love. As Desi was getting ready to depart he noted wryly, "This girl is going to have a hell of a time with that story."

"Why?" asked Lucy.

"Because I have everything arranged to marry you tomorrow morning, if you would like to marry me."

"Where?"

"In Connecticut."

"You're kidding, right?" said Lucy.

"No, I'm not kidding. I want to marry you and I want to marry you tomorrow."

Lucy suggested they just move in together, but Desi wouldn't have it. He had already made arrangements for the marriage license and located a judge who would exempt Connecticut's five-day waiting period.

Early the next morning, Saturday, November 30, 1940, the couple drove to Greenwich, Connecticut. Unfortunately, Desi had forgotten about the blood test, but they managed to squeeze it in before the noon ceremony. Since jewelry stores were closed on the weekend, Desi's manager and agent went to Woolworth's to pick up a ten-cent copper wedding band, which Lucy later had coated in platinum. They were married by a justice of the peace at the Byram River Beagle Club. Due to the wedding, Desi missed his first show at the Roxy that night, but a motorcycle escort took them back to New York, and he made it just in time for his second show.

Four stormy years later, Lucy filed for divorce and was granted an interlocutory decree. But the day before the one-year waiting period for the final decree ended, the couple spent the night together and reconciled.

To reaffirm their love, Desi wanted a second wedding in a Catholic church. So on June 19, 1949, Lucy donned a wedding dress and hat to renew their vows at Our Lady of the Valley Church in Chatsworth, northwest of Los Angeles, with family and friends in attendance.

Two years later, Lucy, still looking for a way to keep her husband at home, suggested to doubting CBS executives that she and Desi play husband and wife on their own television show. At the time, Lucy was portraying a scatterbrained housewife on radio's *My Favorite Husband,* a concept she thought would translate to television. To convince the network that audiences would buy a musical Latin as Lucy's mate, the couple put up the money to produce the pilot. The series was a hit and spawned an industry, Desilu Productions, through which the couple produced many other series. Their daughter Lucie was born in 1951. In 1953, they made another television milestone when Lucy Ricardo gave birth on the air to Little Ricky, the same night that Lucille Ball gave birth to Desi Arnaz IV. Eventually the pressures of their work and personal lives were too much, and Lucy and Desi divorced in 1959.

*The Roman bride, displaying a virgin's reluctance to
leave her family home, kicked and screamed as her new husband carried her over
the threshold on their wedding night.*

Dale Evans and Roy Rogers

Married December 31, 1947

Roy Rogers and Dale Evans were on horseback ready to ride into the spotlight, if not the sunset, when he asked her to marry him. And in perfect keeping with the image of the King of the Cowboys, he did it with a song.

It all began in 1944 when Dale was assigned to her first Roy Rogers feature, *The Cowboy and the Señorita.* A radio, big band and nightclub vocalist, she didn't even know how to ride a horse. But she and Roy "hit it off from the start," reflects Dale today. "I, like his other leading ladies, loved Roy for the responsible, caring person he was." At that time, Roy was married with two small children, and Dale was a single mother with a teenage son, Tom. She had eloped at fourteen and her husband abandoned her when Tom was a baby. When she arrived in Hollywood, the studio instructed Dale to say that Tom was her brother. But, along with Gabby Hayes and the Sons of the Pioneers, Dale says she considered herself part of Roy's "Western family."

Out of their wholesome onscreen relationship – it wasn't Roy's style to kiss his girl – the likable pair scored a radio contract and toured with Roy's troupe on the rodeo circuit.

In 1946, Roy's wife, Arlene, died suddenly from an embolism following the birth of their third child, Roy, Jr. Dale was starring in other pictures when Roy began inviting her to dinner and to drive up to see his children at his ranch by California's Lake Hughes in Ventura County. "We enjoyed being together and had discussed his responsibility for Cheryl, Linda and Roy Jr.," says Dale.

As she explains, "Our courtship grew out of a strong friendship, a long period of working side by side and a deep appreciation of each other." In September of 1947 Roy presented Dale with "a friendship ring."

In October, Dale and Roy were astride their horses in the chutes at the Chicago

Stadium waiting to be announced when Roy suddenly told her he loved her and gave her a star ruby ring. Dale thought it was a birthday present.

But then Roy asked, "What are you doing New Year's Eve?" which was also the title of a popular love song. Dale understood this was a proposal, but she thought he was kidding.

"I am serious," he said.

The announcer called their names, and the couple galloped into the spotlight. On the way, Dale called out, "Let me think about it."

After the show, she sat quietly and prayed. Even though she had always wanted a big family, there were children to consider. She finally gave her answer, yes.

That New Year's Eve, Roy and Dale, both thirty-five, exchanged wedding vows during a blizzard at the Flying L Ranch near Oklahoma City. Roy said his vows in a suit and cowboy boots, and Dale wore a blue wool dress and jacket. Dale used Roy's friendship ring for her wedding ring.

The couple's twenty-six movies and three television series also featured their horses, Buttermilk and Trigger. Although they lost a two-year-old daughter, Roy and Dale adopted four children and fostered another – "the big family I always wanted," says Dale. Their happy trails continue after nearly half a century.

Most professional women, about fifty-five percent, meet their man on the job.

Maria Hawkins and Nat King Cole

Married March 28, 1948

Nat King Cole could melt hearts when he sang, but Maria Hawkins' wasn't dissolving. She wasn't even intrigued by him at first, even though he was already a bona fide star whose King Cole Trio was booked in all the country's top clubs, appeared in movies and racked up many hit songs.

"I think I was standing backstage the first time I heard him. I thought, gee, that's a good trio, but there was no particular thrill. I fell in love with the man," recalls Maria.

It was the summer of 1946, and Nat, twenty-seven, was substituting for the Mills Brothers at Club Zanzibar in New York. Sharing the bill was an attractive young singer known as Maria Ellington who was making her first appearance as a single after having worked as a vocalist in Duke Ellington's band.

Née Maria Hawkins, she wasn't related to Duke, but had been married to a fighter pilot with the same name who was killed the year before. Maria, twenty-three, was raised with every advantage by an aunt who ran a prestigious private school in North Carolina. To please her aunt, Maria dutifully attended Boston Clerical College for three years, but what she really wanted to do was become a torch singer.

Nat, who was so busy playing the piano with his own groups that he never graduated from high school, was instantly enchanted by the refined and well-educated Maria. He was, however, married. Nat's professional good fortunes and uninterrupted life on the road had forced a wedge between him and the woman he married when he was still a teenager. She remained back in Los Angeles. Their marriage was childless, and Nat was crazy about children. Every night he stood backstage and admired Maria in her form-fitting, royal blue sequined gown as she performed her two numbers.

He couldn't take his eyes off her, but every one of his moves was rebuffed. When he sent over champagne, she returned it. When he tried to make conversation with her, he stumbled and failed. When he ran into her backstage, she ignored him.

Maria was completely focused on work. "He was really overly attentive to me, but at the time I wasn't interested. I can truthfully say I was more interested in my career, and that was my first job as a single," she says.

After two weeks of rejection, Nat finally decided to send his valet over to Maria to offer her a ringside ticket to the Joe Louis-Billy Conn fight, a huge event that everyone in New York, including Maria, wanted to attend. She finally said yes. Perhaps he couldn't take the thought of any more brush-offs, but Nat then informed her he wouldn't be joining her. He would give her the ticket and she could sit with Eddie "Rochester" Anderson's wife, Mamie. Maria was thrilled beyond words, and suddenly took notice of the shy, sensitive man. The next day when he asked her to go to the races, she was willing. There, she parlayed a two-dollar bet on a gray horse and won forty dollars. The courtship was off and running.

Maria thought Nat behaved nothing like the seductive crooner he was onstage. "He was a very gentle person, a sweet man. He came over like that to anyone. He was a nice individual, not rough at all, and rather shy when it came to women. He was a man's man, very popular with other guys. He loved sports, and his music came first."

They began going out for dinner together after they were through with work. After a few weeks, shortly before he awkwardly broke the news to her, she found out he was married. They were sitting in his car watching a sunrise when he turned and told her he loved her, but that he had a wife. Against her better judgment, and that of her family, Maria was becoming involved with a married musician.

A few months after meeting Maria, he took her by surprise over dinner at a Chinese restaurant in New York.

"If I can get my divorce, will you marry me?" he asked.

"I had lamb chops in my mouth," recalls Maria. "I didn't even wait until I finished chewing, I just nodded."

The couple had to wait a long time until his divorce was finalized. In the meantime, Nat bought Maria a two-carat round diamond engagement ring at Van Cleef & Arpels. Nat had a wedding ring custom-made, set with marquis-shaped diamonds.

At 4 p.m. on March 28, Easter Sunday, 1948, Congressman Adam Clayton Powell married the couple at the Abyssinian Baptist Church before a crowd of nearly three thousand people, including many musical stars. *Life* magazine reported that the wedding was the biggest and grandest Harlem had seen in decades. As a widow, Maria wore a pale blue satin gown and carried a bouquet of white roses. Nat wore a morning suit. Bill "Bojangles" Robinson's wife, Elaine, and Evelyn Ellington, Duke's daughter-in-law, were among Maria's six bridesmaids. The day following the wedding reception at the Belmont Plaza Hotel, the Coles left for a Mexican honeymoon. While they were away, Nat's recording of "Nature Boy" became a number-one hit. They had three daughters, Natalie, twins Casey and Timolin, an adopted son, Kelly, and an adopted daughter, Carol, who was Maria's niece. Nat died seventeen years later.

In 1993 in Las Vegas, the world's best bet for a quick wedding, an average of two hundred thirty-seven marriage licenses were issued every day — that is, one every six minutes.

Jehan Safwat Raouf and Anwar Sadat

Married May 29, 1949

At fifteen, Jehan Safwat Raouf was fascinated with politics, obsessed with devotion to her native Egypt. When she met Anwar Sadat, a 30-year-old revolutionary whom no one suspected would one day be President of the United Arab Republic, she was in awe. Days later, they were in love; months later they were married.

In the summer of 1948, other girls her age were giddy over movie stars and crooners, but Jehan was devoted to national news and the salvation of her homeland from the dominance of the British. She was infatuated with Captain Anwar el-Sadat, who had been on trial for eight months for the political assassination of the Egyptian traitor Amin Osman, the country's Minister of Finance. Osman had been a champion of ties between Egypt and the colonial British. Anwar had been dismissed from the army and imprisoned for two years during World War II for his clandestine activities with the Germans to weaken British control. In 1944, he escaped and lived in hiding until the war ended. A year later, after forming an underground organization dedicated to ridding Egypt of collaborators, he was arrested for Osman's murder.

Anwar was everything Jehan longed to be – a patriot and an activist. Trapped by the cultural limitations placed on women, Jehan did what she could to spread the word of liberation among her family and friends. She followed every news article about Sadat, desperate for word of her hero's fate. And she prayed daily, sometimes hourly for his safety. On the very day that she had breathlessly run three miles into town to find a paper and read that he had finally been acquitted, a miracle happened.

She was staying with relatives in Suez to celebrate Ramadan, the sacred ninth month of the Islamic year in which fasting occurs between dawn and dusk. She and Auntie Zouzou were slicing mango for *suhur,* the meal eaten just before sunrise, when her cousin's husband, Hassan Izzat, announced that a friend had arrived for a visit. It was Anwar el-Sadat.

No one could have predicted a romance. He was divorcing his first wife, the mother of their three children. He was fifteen years her senior. He had very dark skin, which was looked down upon in her culture. He had no money. And besides, Jehan's parents were already making plans to arrange her marriage to someone they felt was suitable.

Arranged marriages were customary in the strict Muslim society in which she was brought up in Cairo. Jehan's father, Safwat Raouf, had defied convention when he rejected the cousin his parents had selected as his bride and married an English-woman, Gladys Cotrell, a Christian who never converted to Islam and who always ate British food. Nevertheless, Jehan's parents were considering three boys as prospective husbands, including Hassan Izzat's brother. There would be a wedding in about two years when Jehan turned seventeen. "It was unusual to fall in love and have a romantic story," Jehan recalls.

Within two days of meeting Anwar, she was infatuated. He too was enraptured with the young girl to whom he was soon pouring out his heart, sharing his hopes and dreams. To her amazement, when he learned she had just had a birthday, he offered to sing her a love song. They spent the next several days talking, often chaperoned by Jehan's cousin Aida who volunteered to sit with the couple so they could dine, almost tête-à-tête.

"We fell in love together – it was something magic between us," says Jehan, who could barely wait for him to propose. When he did, it was less than a month after they met. The words, which neither of them preserved, were in verse that conveyed his love for her. He told her that he wanted to speak to her father and mother and be formally engaged.

Anwar was penniless, so Hassan suggested that they lie and tell her father that her intended was extremely rich. "Never, I will never cheat your father," said Anwar, protesting the deception. But Jehan urged him to go along with it and promised to reveal the truth before they were married. "I am the one who is going to marry you, not my father, but they will not agree if they know that you are poor," she asserted. He reluctantly agreed.

Hassan pleaded Anwar's case to her parents. "My cousin told my father, 'He is extremely rich. He has ranches,' " recalls Jehan. While her father disapproved of Anwar's politics, he was more amenable to Anwar than her mother. Gladys was adamant that Anwar was too old; furthermore, no one in their family had ever married a divorced man.

Jehan was too respectful of her parents to marry without their approval, so she lobbied for her mother's blessing. "I insisted," says Jehan. "I was not going to change my mind. I begged her sometimes. Sometimes I cried."

They finally agreed to meet Anwar. But when he talked about his disdain for

Winston Churchill, the British-born Gladys was hardly impressed. During their second meeting, however, he won her over. This time, Jehan coached him, "Talk about books. She is British. Most of her time is spent reading." When he mentioned his fondness for Dickens, Gladys saw that he was a man of substance and character and finally gave her consent. Safwat gave his approval on the condition that Anwar never again engage in politics. Anwar agreed.

During the engagement, Jehan told her father the truth about Anwar's finances. "He said, 'I knew it,' " she recalls. "But he knew I loved him so much." Safwat help-ed Anwar pay for Jehan's two gold engagement rings, one shaped like a butterfly. Anwar couldn't afford to buy her a second piece of jewelry, which was typical for an Egyptian engagement. Nor could he pay the dowry dictated by the Koran. "All our lives I teased him, 'You married me very cheap,' " she says.

Six months later, on May 29, 1949, Jehan prepared for her wedding day by the cen-turies-old Middle Eastern custom of removing the hair from arms and legs with a hot paste of lemon and sugar. Jehan wore a long white gown that she designed herself and held a bouquet of roses, jasmine and iris. Anwar wore his military uniform.

Because of her age, Jehan could only sit in the same room as Anwar during the marriage ceremony at her parents' house. It was her father who clasped hands with Anwar before a sheikh. The sheikh asked Safwat if Jehan accepted Anwar as her hus-band. "Yes," said Jehan. "She consents," said Safwat. The party at Auntie Zouzou's home featured belly dancers, musicians, a comedian and three dancing horses.

Later that night the couple drove to the Pyramids and the Sphinx and contem-plated their future life together and their love of Egypt. They honeymooned in Zagazig, located in the delta between Cairo and Alexandria.

During another drive to the Pyramids, Anwar said, "Jehan, you remember, I promised your father that I will not be involved in politics."

"Anwar," she reminded him, "You are not marrying my father, you are marrying me. And I love you because you are devoted to Egypt. I am the one my father took the promise for. I release you from the promise because I want you as brave as you are and I love you this way." The couple had three daughters, Loubna, Noha and Jehan, who were born in 1954, 1958 and 1961, respectively, and one son, Gamal, born in 1956.

Thirty-two years after the couple was married, on October 6, 1981, Jehan stood a few feet behind her husband, with two of her grandchildren at her sides, as they watched President Anwar Sadat – the man she had loved for what seemed like forever – be killed by assassins' bullets. She turned to Vice-President Hosni Mubarak and said, "Mr. President, you'll have to take over now. It's Egypt now that we have to face. Sadat is over."

Nancy Davis and Ronald Reagan

Married March 4, 1952

"God must think a lot of me to have given me you," Ronald Reagan often told Nancy Davis when they were courting. It was a line he borrowed from his role as pitcher Grover Cleveland Alexander in the 1952 movie *The Winning Team*. Hearing those words forty years later still brings tears to Nancy's eyes. And when it came to proposing, she says, her romantic suitor never needed words. She always knew they would be a winning team someday.

It all began in Hollywood, during the fall of 1949. Nancy, née Anne Frances Robbins, daughter of a stage actress and stepdaughter of a prominent Chicago neurosurgeon, was a fledgling actress under contract to Metro-Goldwyn-Mayer. She had been receiving mail from left-wing organizations that was obviously meant for another Nancy Davis. She was especially concerned when her name appeared on a list of Communist sympathizers in a Hollywood trade paper, and turned to Mervyn LeRoy, who was directing a movie in which she had a small part.

He volunteered to check with Ronald, who was president of the Screen Actors Guild. "I said, 'Oh yes, by all means do that,' " remembers Nancy. She found him extremely attractive on screen. Divorced from Jane Wyman for more than a year, the popular leading man was a highly eligible bachelor.

Ronald reported back to the director that there were four or five Nancy Davises working in Hollywood, only one of whom was an actress. He promised that if she ever had any problems, the guild would handle them on her behalf.

"I didn't think that should be the end of it," admits Nancy, who was frankly interested in meeting Ronald. When Mervyn told her, "Come to think of it, I think you two would like to know each other," she agreed wholeheartedly, and Mervyn put in another call, this time suggesting a blind date. When Nancy hadn't heard from Ronald after two days, she stood next to Mervyn while he telephoned again.

Ronald finally made the call, but to protect himself from a potentially unpleasant evening, he asked her out for an early dinner, saying he had a pre-dawn call on the set the next day.

"I said, 'That's perfectly all right, because I have an early morning call, too,' which I didn't at all," recalls Nancy.

Their dinner date at La Rue, an elegant French restaurant on the Sunset Strip, was much more pleasant than Ronald had expected. He asked Nancy if she wanted to catch Sophie Tucker's show at Ciro's.

She accepted, but only if they could see the first show – "because a girl's gotta have some pride," she explains today.

When the early show extended into the late show, both admitted they didn't have morning appointments after all.

For the next six months, they saw each other regularly while continuing to date others. Ronald was slow to make a commitment, having been through one marriage already.

"He was very gun-shy," says Nancy. "He'd been burned once and didn't want to get burned again, and I didn't want to get burned at all." But Nancy knew right away that "Ronnie" was the one for her. "He was unlike any actor I'd ever known. It wasn't about my next picture or my last picture. He had interests beyond the movies."

In his spare time, Ronald went horseback riding at his small ranch in the San Fernando Valley, his private retreat. The first time he invited Nancy along, she knew she had "made progress." When he finally invited her to meet his children, she thought, "Oh my, that's really a step forward." However she also realized that if she was going to get anywhere with him, she'd better get over her fear of horses and agreed to let him give her riding lessons. To spend more time with Ronald, Nancy also got involved with the guild, and she was eventually appointed to the board.

Since neither particularly enjoyed the nightclub scene, they often dined at the home of their closest friends, Ardis and William Holden, or alone at Chasen's, their favorite hangout, huddled in the third booth to the left in the front room.

By Christmas 1951 they both knew the relationship was solidified. Ronald asked Nancy not to go home to Chicago, but to spend the holiday with him and his children. Marriage talk commenced, but after a long dry spell in his career, Ronald had been cast to star in three movies back to back – *The Winning Team, Hong Kong* and *She's Working Her Way Through College*. In February 1952, over dinner at Chasen's, they set the date and made plans. Ronald called Nancy's stepfather to ask for her hand.

At the next Screen Actors Guild meeting, Ronald wrote a note to Bill Holden asking him to be his best man. "About time," Bill wrote back.

The couple planned a secret, late-afternoon wedding ceremony at the Little Brown Church in the San Fernando Valley on March 4, 1952. Nancy wore a gray suit with white collar and cuffs and a small, veiled hat. Best man Holden and Ardis, Nancy's matron of honor, were the only guests. Because Ronald couldn't afford to buy Nancy two rings, they picked out a diamond wedding band from Ruser's on Rodeo Drive in Beverly Hills.

After the ceremony, the Reagans went to dinner at the Holdens' North Hollywood home, joined by the Holdens' two sons. After cutting the cake, the bride and groom drove to the Mission Inn in Riverside, southeast of Los Angeles. The next day they continued their drive to Phoenix to be with Nancy's parents. "I think we're probably the only people who spent their honeymoon with their family," says Nancy.

Soon after, she asked to be released from her seven-year studio contract so she could devote herself to her husband and family, which included a daughter, Patti, and son, Ron.

Coretta Scott and Martin Luther King, Jr.

Married June 18, 1953

Coretta Scott wasn't keen about going out with a minister. Based on those she knew back home, men of the cloth were far too provincial and "overly pious," as she put it. So meeting a Baptist preacher named Martin Luther King, Jr. – especially on a blind date – was less than thrilling to her. She wanted a man as intelligent and as committed to the civil rights cause as she was. When the preacher broached the subject of marriage on that first date in January 1952, her guard went up immediately.

Indeed, Coretta agreed to meet Martin out of courtesy to her friend Mary Powell, a fellow student at the New England Conservatory of Music who had arranged the set-up. Mary had told her that twenty-three-year-old "M.L." was an outstanding catch – so Coretta was at least curious. Mary knew Martin from their college days in Atlanta, and she often ran into him at the Western Lunch Box, a soul-food restaurant popular with Boston college students. He complained that he was lonely for southern girls because northern girls were too "reserved." Mary suggested two southern girls she knew, but Martin had already met one of them. Mary wasn't sure if Coretta was devout enough for him, but she gave him her phone number.

After graduating from Antioch College with degrees in education and music, Coretta went on to the conservatory in Boston with hopes of becoming a concert singer. She had also come north to escape the racism and segregation she and her family had faced on a regular basis throughout her childhood in Marion, Alabama. Her father, Obadiah, was the only African-American in town to own a truck, then three trucks. He struggled and saved to buy a small sawmill. Two weeks after he bought it, he found it burned to ashes; he went back to hauling. Coretta would never forget the sorrow and the outrage she felt.

Ensconced in an intellectual community, Coretta, twenty-four, found herself re-evaluating her philosophical underpinnings. She didn't know it then, she says today, but she was looking internally for an accepting and universal religion – exactly what Martin preached. At the time she thought Baptist doctrine was too rigid and believed that her baptism by sprinkling in her Methodist church was as valid as the Baptists' baptism by immersion.

Martin's calling seemed clear early on. His maternal grandfather, Adam Daniel Williams, was the pastor of Ebenezer Baptist Church, one of the nuclei of Atlanta's black ghetto. Upon Williams' death, Martin's father, Martin Sr., succeeded him as pastor. Daddy King – Martin's father – was a strong presence in his life. Martin Jr. followed in his footsteps and was ordained as a minister at eighteen, before his senior year at Morehouse College in Atlanta. He continued his studies at Crozer Theological Seminary before going to Boston University to earn his doctorate.

As soon as Martin picked up Coretta for their first date, lunch at Sharaf's Restaurant, he liked what he saw. She was a pretty woman with long hair and bangs. The first thing Coretta noticed about Martin was that he was short and not terribly handsome. However, when he started talking, she began to find him extremely appealing and magnetic. Coretta liked his focus and self-confidence, but nothing could have prepared her for what came next.

After lunch, Martin drove her back to the conservatory and said, "Do you know something?"

"What is that?"

"You have everything I have ever wanted in a wife. There are only four things, and you have them all."

"I don't see how you can say that. You don't even know me."

"Yes, I can tell," he said. "The four things that I look for in a wife are character, intelligence, personality and beauty. And you have them all. I want to see you again. When can I?"

"I don't know," said Coretta. "I'll have to check my schedule. You may call me later."

This was all happening much too quickly. Coretta was intent on pursuing her career and wasn't even thinking about getting married now. Besides, as genuine as Martin seemed, his sudden proposal aroused her suspicions. When he called the next day for a date, she told him she might see him *if* her date cancelled. Determined, he called back Saturday at four in the afternoon; she was free.

Soon, Coretta learned that Martin was thoughtful and polite. They continued to see each other that winter, frequently discussing philosophy, religion and the condition of black Americans. Coretta was deeply moved when she went to listen to Martin preach. They weren't always serious, though. They both liked to dance and listen to music.

Martin was ready to find a wife and often talked marriage with Coretta. He had been unofficially engaged to a girl from Atlanta whose parents were close to his, but she was more his parents' choice than his. He was looking for a woman who would be by his side as pastor of the Ebenezer Church. He needed a woman who would be home for him and not thinking about her own career.

Coretta knew she wanted a husband and children, but she still had several reservations. She had worked hard to earn her position at the conservatory. She didn't know how comfortable she'd be in the role of a minister's wife. And she worried that Daddy King favored the girl in Atlanta for his son. She prayed for help.

Over the summer, Martin invited Coretta to visit him and his family in Atlanta. As a sort of test, to see if he truly cared about her, Coretta refused. Martin, hurt and angry, told her the relationship was off. Coretta quickly backed down, and in August she took the train to Atlanta. As she feared, Daddy King was a little cool. He still considered Martin's other girl the ideal wife for his son.

A few months later, in November, Martin's mother, Alberta, and father, visited him in Boston. Martin, Coretta and his parents were all in his apartment when Daddy King, unaware that the pair was serious, started complaining that his son had dated some of the finest girls, but never seemed interested in them. Coretta was frustrated that Martin didn't speak out in her behalf. Finally, Martin went in another room and told his mother, not his father, that he was going to marry Coretta.

Two days later, Daddy King came to visit again. Pounding his hand on the table, he cried out: "You all are courting too hard. What's this doing to your studies?"

"I'm going on to get my doctorate, and then I'm going to marry Coretta," said Martin.

"What about you, Coretta? How are you getting on at the conservatory?" asked Daddy King.

"I'm getting on all right," she said, "but it is difficult."

"That's what I thought. Now you two had better get married," he said firmly.

Coretta had decided that Martin was her priority now and was willing to forego singing for wherever life at his side would lead her. She changed her major to musical education. The couple soon announced their engagement.

On June 18, 1953, Daddy King married Martin and Coretta in the garden of her parents' home in Marion. Coretta didn't want to wear a traditional long white gown. Instead, she wore a pale-blue ankle-length dress with matching gloves and shoes. Martin wore a white double-breasted dinner jacket. Coretta helped cook the Southern-style dinner. Daddy King agreed to delete the section of the bride's vows about promising to obey.

Since there were no local hotels and those nearest didn't allow blacks, the couple spent their first night together at the home of her family's undertaker. They continued on to Atlanta where the King family hosted a reception.

After they were married, Coretta became a Baptist and was baptized by immersion. They had four children: Yolanda Denise, born in 1955, Martin Luther III, 1957, Dexter Scott, 1961, and Bernice Albertine, 1963.

Jacqueline Bouvier and John Fitzgerald Kennedy

Married September 12, 1953

It took a mutual friend three years to finally introduce John Fitzgerald Kennedy, a handsome and popular young congressman from Boston's blue-collar Eleventh District, to Jacqueline Bouvier, an aristocratic and stylish beauty working for a Washington newspaper. Charles Bartlett didn't realize he was creating a twosome so magical that as America's President and First Lady they would lead a White House era likened to Camelot and captivate the country for generations.

Jackie "always had these sort of English beaux, and I must say they were not up to her," recalled Bartlett, then Washington correspondent for the *Chattanooga Times*. Jack, meanwhile, six feet tall with thick brown hair that was always falling over one eyebrow, had a well-earned reputation as a ladies' man and was often photographed on the nightclub rounds with one glamour girl or another on his arm.

The match clearly had potential. Like Jack, Jackie was from a wealthy Catholic family, and was someone his powerful clan would surely welcome. Indeed, with his famous Massachusetts name, money (his father, Joseph P. Kennedy, had endowed each of his children with one million dollars when they reached voting age) and good looks, Jack was considered by many to be the most eligible bachelor in the country. Never mind Jack's political future – during his campaign for the U.S. Senate, the *Saturday Evening Post* reported that "every women wanted either to mother him or marry him." By then, Jackie had fallen into the latter category.

Bartlett's first attempt to acquaint the two, in 1948, at his brother's wedding in Long Island, was a flop. He tried to engineer Jackie across a crowded room to meet Jack, but at about the halfway point, he introduced her to the boxer Gene Tunney, with whom she began a conversation. By the time he got her to the other side of the room, Jack had already left.

Though the fix-up was "always in his mind," Bartlett didn't succeed until he and his wife, Martha, gave a small dinner party at their Georgetown home in the spring of 1951. By that time, Jackie had spent a year at the Sorbonne in Paris and was enrolled at George Washington University in Washington, D.C. During her short time in the capital she had also been briefly engaged to stockbroker John Husted.

Not surprisingly, the future president was attracted to his dinner companion. "I leaned across the asparagus and asked for a date," he recounted. After dinner, Bartlett remembered walking her to her car and Jack chasing after her. "He was muttering shyly about, 'Shall we go someplace and have a drink?'" recalled Bartlett. Somehow, a friend of hers had been waiting for her in her car. She had to pass on the drink.

"It was a very spasmodic courtship," Jackie said. "We didn't see each other for six months, because I went to Europe again and Jack began his summer and fall campaigning in Massachusetts. Then came six months when we were both back. Jack was in Congress, and I was in my last year of George Washington University. But it was still spasmodic because he spent half of each week in Massachusetts."

By now Jack was deep into his campaign. In December of 1952, Martha Bartlett decided to intervene. She needed an extra male guest for a dinner party she was giving, and she told Jackie, now the "Inquiring Photographer" for the *Washington Times-Herald,* to invite Jack.

During the weeks that followed, the two went to the movies together – Jack particularly enjoyed Westerns and movies about the Civil War – and they discussed the history books he gave her, including Marquis James' *The Raven* and John Buchan's *Pilgrim's Way*. In return, Jackie gave him two books of her own drawings. There was at least one subject they didn't discuss. "We hardly every talked politics," said Jackie.

Jack asked her to accompany him to President Dwight Eisenhower's inaugural ball the following month. In May, Jackie was on assignment in London and preparing to photograph the coronation of Queen Elizabeth II. Contrary to many accounts, Jack didn't propose while Jackie was overseas by either telephone or telegram. The telegram that he did send her, however, was a declaration of sorts: "Articles excellent but you are missed." Indeed, when she returned, he asked for her hand in marriage. To seal the betrothal, Jackie received a square-cut diamond-and-emerald ring from Van Cleef & Arpels. They waited until June 25 to announce their engagement, supposedly to avoid contradicting a just-published *Saturday Evening Post* profile entitled "Jack Kennedy – The Senate's Gay Young Bachelor."

The coronation of Queen Elizabeth in Great Britain was a suitable preamble to the thirty-six-year-old senator's storybook wedding on September 12, 1953, less than a decade before he was elected the thirty-fifth president of the United States. The wedding was considered the most impressive social gathering that the denizens of Newport, Rhode Island, had witnessed in thirty years, the details of which were breathlessly covered by *Life* magazine.

Archbishop Richard Cushing of Boston performed the rites and read a special blessing from Pope Pius XII at St. Mary's Roman Catholic Church while some five hundred fifty guests, including diplomats and senators (the entire Senate was invited), looked on. Jackie, twenty-four, wore a demure pearl choker, her grandmother's lace veil, a tiara of orange blossoms and a gown stitched from fifty yards of cream faille. Holding fast to bridal tradition of wearing something borrowed and something blue, she clutched her mother's lace handkerchief and wore a blue garter. Jack wore a morning suit. His brother, Robert, was his best man. Jackie's sister, Lee Bouvier Canfield, was matron of honor. At the last minute, her father, Jack Bouvier, reportedly fell ill, and her stepfather, Hugh D. Auchincloss, escorted her down the aisle.

Twelve hundred guests attended a reception at Hammersmith Farm, the three-hundred-acre estate on Narragansett Bay belonging to Jackie's stepfather and her mother, Janet. The newlyweds spent nearly two hours greeting guests before everyone sat down to their fruit cups under a massive striped tent erected on the lawn. The fifteen-piece Meyer Davis Society Band played. The couple spent the night at the Waldorf-Astoria in Manhattan and then honeymooned in Acapulco before checking into a hillside suite at San Ysidro Ranch in Montecito, California. After Jackie suffered a miscarriage and a still-born birth, their daughter, Caroline, was born four years later, November 27, 1957, followed by sons, John, Jr., born November 25, 1960, and Patrick who was born in 1963 during his father's presidency but lived only 39 hours. The child was the first baby born to an incumbent U.S. president since 1895.

Marilyn Monroe and Joe DiMaggio

Married January 14, 1954

The marriage of America's favorite blonde and the Yankee Clipper lasted a mere nine months, but together they symbolized America's conflicting appetites for sex and apple pie. Even long after the marriage was over, it was difficult to think of Marilyn Monroe without Joe DiMaggio.

The momentous blind date that brought them together occurred in June 1952. David March, a friend and business manager, was credited with playing Cupid. Marilyn's career was on a meteoric rise at 20th Century-Fox, where she was making *Monkey Business*. Joe, who was the most celebrated baseball player since Babe Ruth, had retired the year before. Yet for all their success and fame, they were both kind of shy. Both had limited educations. Joe came from a big, close-knit Italian family. Marilyn grew up in foster homes and yearned for the stability of a family she never had.

But Joe was a straight arrow, and Marilyn was the type who would happily lean over to accommodate a photographer in search of cheesecake. Perhaps because he had been famous most of his life, Joe shunned the spotlight – but with Marilyn around, that's all there ever was. Marilyn wasn't exactly the girl next door.

Both were unattached when they met. Marilyn's former lover, William Morris Agency honcho Johnny Hyde, was dead. Joe was divorced from showgirl Dorothy Arnold, with whom he had a son.

During their courtship, Joe was doing commentary for the Yankees' home games and flew to Los Angeles to see Marilyn whenever his schedule was free. Marilyn had finally risen above forgettable bit parts and was appearing in one film after another, on her way to becoming 20th Century-Fox's biggest star.

Despite conflicting schedules, they made efforts to see each other, much to the public's delight. While Marilyn was on location at the Falls filming *Niagara*, Joe visited her. There was gleeful speculation that they would elope. Sometimes she joined Joe on trips to his hometown, San Francisco. In Los Angeles, they avoided the Hollywood nightclub scene, preferring to stay in and make spaghetti in Marilyn's apartment on Doheny Drive. Joe liked to fish and Marilyn went along. They became stay-at-home types, but even at home, their styles varied – Joe liked television, Marilyn was educating herself with books.

Nearly two years after they met, the couple arranged a secret civil marriage ceremony in San Francisco at 1:45 p.m. on January 14, 1954 in the chambers of Municipal Judge Charles S. Perry. The secret got out: crowds formed outside City Hall.

Marilyn, sporting a three-carat solitaire diamond engagement ring, promised to "love, honor and cherish," but not obey, Joe, thirty-nine. The bride wore a buttoned-up dark brown suit with an ermine collar, because Joe liked her in conservative clothing. She signed her name to the wedding license as Norma Jean Dougherty – a reminder of her ill-fated teenage marriage to Jim Dougherty, an aircraft plant worker. She gave her age as twenty-five. She was actually twenty-eight.

A few of Joe's relatives and friends attended, though no one from Marilyn's side came. After the ceremony, Joe informed the congregating reporters angling for the prenuptial scoop, "We have been thinking it over for some time. We decided two nights ago when we had a birthday party for Dom," referring to his brother.

Marilyn offered that she wanted six children. Joe said, "We'll have at least one." In retrospect, their differences were evident even then.

After the wedding, they spent the night at a motel in Paso Robles, California, on their way to Palm Springs. They had another sort of honeymoon planned in Japan. Intimate it was not. They went with Joe's mentor, Frank "Lefty" O'Doul, who had coached Joe in the minor leagues, and his bride Jean. The two sports stars were there on baseball business. Yet no matter where Marilyn and Joe went, Marilyn grabbed attention. At their Tokyo press conference, an Associated Press reporter remarked, "While Miss Monroe talked to approximately seventy-five newsmen, DiMaggio was almost unnoticed in a corner of the room."

The public tracked the romance avidly. "Mr. and Mrs. America, and Junior and Miss too, followed the pair like DiMaggio at the plate used to follow the flight of a curve ball," a reporter wrote in the *Los Angeles Herald Express*. While they were overseas, Marilyn was asked to stop in Korea to visit American troops. She couldn't say no, and left Joe with his friends in Tokyo. More Marilyn headlines, more reporters.

When she returned, she said excitedly, "Joe, you never heard such cheering."

DiMaggio responded glumly, "Yes, I have."

In October, at a press conference at their rented Beverly Hills home, Marilyn announced that she was filing for divorce. "It's all on account of our careers," she said.

And yet, following her divorce from playwright Arthur Miller, Joe and Marilyn re-established a close friendship. After Marilyn died of an apparent suicide at age thirty-six in 1962, Joe sobbed throughout her funeral service at the Westwood Village Mortuary. He sent roses to her gravesite three times a week for twenty years.

June is the most popular month to wed.
The least popular is January.

Grace Kelly and
His Serene Highness Prince Rainier III of Monaco

Married April 19, 1956

Prince of pint-sized, though enchanting, European principality weds beautiful and patrician American movie star. It was the fairy tale of the '50s, and Grace Kelly, true to her name and promise, played her greatest role with dignity and style for almost three decades, until her fatal automobile accident in 1982.

It began in May 1955, when Grace, in the south of France to attend the Cannes Film Festival, agreed to pose for a *Paris Match* photo layout with His Serene Highness Prince Rainier III of Monaco. They had never met, though Grace had visited the palace during the making of Alfred Hitchcock's *To Catch a Thief* a year earlier.

The twenty-six-year-old movie star was late. The prince, whose thirty-second birthday was a few days off, was even later. The entire photo shoot took forty-five minutes. While a photographer recorded the event, the stocky, mustached prince escorted the serene, Philadelphia-bred beauty through the gardens and his small, exotic zoo.

But lightning didn't strike. Grace, apparently, was preoccupied. While in Cannes, she had several romantic encounters with French actor Jean-Pierre Aumont, which caused far more of a media stir than her tour with Rainier and his tigers.

Rainier, who succeeded his grandfather in 1949, had ended his long and serious affair with French actress Gisele Pascal. Reportedly they parted because she was unable to bear children and produce an heir (although later she married and defied nature by having a child). Marriage and babies weighed heavily on Rainier's mind: A 1918 treaty between Monaco and France stipulated that Monaco would be recognized as an independent principality as long as the throne was occupied, otherwise the country would revert to France. Rainier's sister, Princess Antoinette, had renounced her claim to the throne. Thus, it was left to Rainier to produce an heir.

It was unlikely the prince and the movie star would ever meet again. In the fall, she was heading off to Asheville, North Carolina, where she would begin filming *The Swan*, ironically the story of a noble girl whose mother wants her to marry a prince. But Cupid was served a few months later by Father Francis Tucker, an American chaplain formerly with a Philadelphia parish, who was assigned by the Vatican to the parish of St. Charles in Monaco.

His accomplices were friends of Grace's family, "Aunt" Edie and "Uncle" Russ Austin, who were vacationing on the French Riviera. Unable to obtain tickets to the Sporting Club Gala in Monte Carlo, they audaciously called the palace on a whim to see if Rainier could help, mentioning that they were friends of Grace Kelly's.

Father Tucker returned their call to say that Rainier had not only secured the couple a front table at the event, but invited them for tea the next day. It seems the priest took it upon himself to play matchmaker for his prince and the Catholic actress. The tea ended with the Austins asking Rainier to drop by next time he was in Margate, New Jersey.

A short time later, Father Tucker contacted the Austins again, this time announcing that Rainier was traveling to the United States in December, supposedly for a routine check-up at Johns Hopkins University Hospital in Baltimore.

As promised, Rainier, Father Tucker and a young doctor dined at the Austins', and then an invitation was arranged for the little group to join the Kelly family at their home for Christmas Eve dinner. The second meeting between the prince and the star went more than smoothly. After dinner, Grace and Rainier went on to her sister Peggy Kelly Davis' house. By the time they returned to the Kellys', it was practically morning, and Rainier ended up spending the night in one of the Kellys' guest rooms. Over the next few days, Rainier and Grace saw each other constantly, in both Philadelphia and New York. And, perhaps in Grace's spacious Fifth Avenue apartment, Rainier asked for her hand.

Rainier denied that the proposal was impetuous. "I think we were both ready for marriage," he said. Although Grace had her share of flings with Hollywood leading men and an on-again-off-again relationship with fashion designer Oleg Cassini, she had often told friends that she wanted to marry and have children.

On December 28, Grace started to let the word out – she and Rainier were engaged. He gave her a friendship ring, a band with diamonds and rubies, until her twelve-carat emerald-cut diamond engagement ring could be made up.

The Kellys hoped to have the wedding on their turf at St. Bridget's Church, site of Grace's first communion, but they acquiesced to Rainier's wishes for the wedding to take place in Monaco's Cathedral of St. Nicholas, where his forebears had married.

A few days later, Grace left for Los Angeles to start work on her last film, *High Society*. In the middle of filming, she switched the prop-department diamond ring that her character, socialite Tracy Lord, wears for her big new diamond. Later in January, Rainier and his father, Prince Pierre, followed her to L.A., renting a house in Bel-Air for several weeks.

Grace still had several years remaining on her MGM contract. While most of Hollywood couldn't believe that she would relinquish her phenomenal movie career, Rainier wasn't about to have his bride commuting to Hollywood. MGM agreed to let her out of her obligation to make her next film, *Designing Woman,* based on the life of costume designer Helen Rose, if the studio could have exclusive film rights to the wedding. The studio and Monaco agreed to a fifty-fifty split of profits. (Monaco's take would go to the Red Cross.)

Amid the showers and parties and dinners in her and Rainier's honor, Grace studied French, gave interviews and finished making *High Society* in March. She presented Ernest Borgnine with an Oscar for Best Actor in *Marty* at the Academy Awards ceremony and left for New York to be a bridesmaid in the wedding of her former roommate, Rita Gam.

On April 4, Grace and her wedding party of sixty-five boarded the ocean liner *Constitution* for Monaco, as an international conglomeration of photographers, reporters and camera crews chronicled the frenzied send-off. The world awaited every morsel of news about the magical couple whose wedding promised to be a greater spectacle than the coronation of Queen Elizabeth II three years earlier.

Eight days later, Rainier, an avid sailor, greeted his bride-to-be just outside Monaco's harbor aboard the yacht *Deo Juvante II*, his wedding present to her.

The week preceding the wedding was a heady mix of receptions and galas, including one party at which Margot Fonteyn and Christopher Soames danced. After the dinner following the wedding rehearsal, Grace appeared wearing a gift from Rainier's father – a family necklace featuring a huge pearl surrounded by rubies and topped with a small diamond filigree crown.

On the morning of April 18, eighty carefully selected guests watched as Grace, wearing a dress of pale pink taffeta and cream-colored Alencon lace, white kid gloves and a Juliet cap, and Rainier, in a black morning coat, striped trousers, white vest and gray tie, exchanged vows in French (*"Oui,"* they both answered Judge Marcel Portanier) in a civil ceremony in the palace's baroque throne room. That night, at a gala at the Opera House, Grace wore the red and white sash of the Order of St. Charles, Monaco's highest honor, across the chest of her Lanvin ball gown.

At 9:30 a.m. on April 19, diplomats, heads of state, movie stars and socialites, including the Aga Khan, Cary Grant, Ava Gardner, David Niven, Gloria Swanson and Aristotle Onassis – men were dressed in white tie and full dress uniforms – were among the crowd of 600 filling the Cathedral of St. Nicholas to witness the cinematic ceremony with high Mass conducted by the Bishop of Monaco, Monseigneur Gilles Barthe. The altar was brimming with white lilacs, hydrangeas and lilies, and baskets of snapdragons were suspended from chandeliers.

The bride's and groom's families entered the church first. They were followed by six bridesmaids and the matron of honor, Peggy, all dressed in yellow organdy, and six junior attendants – four girls in white dresses and two boys in white satin breeches.

Then came Grace and her father, Jack, for she would await Rainier at the altar. Rainier wore a Monegasque uniform and Grace wore a gown courtesy of MGM's resident costume designer Helen Rose, who was obviously thinking "regal" when she envisioned it. The high-necked, long-sleeved gown was fitted through the torso and erupted into a billowing skirt, a creation composed of hundreds of yards of silk taffeta, peau de soie, tulle and lace. Her head was covered in a Juliet cap decorated with seed pearls and a veil made from some ninety yards of tulle.

Following the ceremony, the couple rode through the tiny principality in a cream-and-black Rolls-Royce convertible, a gift from the people of Monaco. At the Church of Sainte Devote, Princess Grace stepped out of the car to pray at the altar of the patron saint of Monaco. Later, the couple greeted the six hundred wedding guests at a luncheon reception at the palace.

After slicing the wedding cake with Rainier's sword, they boarded the *Deo Juvante II* for a honeymoon cruise, stopping first in Villefranche, then moving on to Spain and Corsica. She tried to be a good sailor but frequently was seasick.

Nine months later, Princess Grace produced, by natural childbirth, a daughter, Princess Caroline Louise Margueritte, on January 23, 1957. Prince Albert Louis Pierre, the heir to the throne, was born the following year on March 14. The couple then had a second daughter, Princess Stéphanie Marie Elisabeth, on February 1, 1965.

*The traditional white wedding dress
first became popular in Victorian times among upper-class brides
who were rich enough to wear a dress only once.*

Beverly Sills and Peter Greenough

Married November 17, 1956

Yes, their eyes met across a crowded room, and cymbals crashed. She says lightning struck on their first date.

But just like the best of operatic lovers, fledgling diva Beverly Sills and newspaper scion Peter Greenough had to navigate the inevitable plot complications before the triumphant wedding march finale.

"It really was an old-fashioned *coup de foudre*. The first time we saw each other, that was it," says Peter, who jotted down his phone number and a request for a date on a matchbook and passed it to the young singer. Beverly wasn't famous, but she was conspicuous, having played up her voluptuousness in a very low-cut dress that night.

The event was a press reception for the Cleveland opening of a touring New York City Opera production of *Die Fledermaus*. It was the weekend before Thanksgiving 1955. Beverly, twenty-six, had been with the company one month and was totally focused on her career. There were few prospects for American opera singers and, after two years of rejections by the company, she knew she was lucky to be given the role of Rosalinda. Peter, thirteen years her senior, was associate editor of the *Cleveland Plain Dealer,* the newspaper that his family owned.

Beverly found Peter "absolutely gorgeous." He beseeched her to stay another day so they could get to know each other. But Beverly, who was sharing a one-bedroom apartment in Manhattan with her mother, was a good daughter. She knew her mother was expecting her home and didn't want to worry her. "I never changed my travel plans," she recollects. "Never." But this time she made an exception.

On the first date, Peter arrived at Beverly's hotel with two girls, ages six and nine.

"Who are these two little things and where is their mother?" asked Beverly.

"They're mine. I sued her for divorce and got custody yesterday," he replied.

Beverly's first inclination was, "I better get out of here." And she didn't even know that a third child was at home asleep.

By the end of their date in Peter's palatial, French-style mansion on Lake Erie, both felt as if they'd "been hit by thunder and lightning," says Beverly.

The next weekend, and every weekend thereafter, Peter flew to New York to court Beverly. He also had to woo Beverly's mother, Shirley Silverman, by arriving with armloads of flowers, books and presents.

Beverly's mother was totally against the relationship. Peter, a Protestant, was hardly every Jewish mother's dream. Besides, he was still married.

There were problems from Peter's family as well. He came from a long line of Boston Brahmins whose ancestors dated directly back to John Alden. The Greenoughs were so opposed to the idea of his dating a Jewish girl from Brooklyn that they didn't even want to meet her.

But nothing daunted Peter. "Do you think you could ever live in Cleveland?" he asked Beverly over dinner at a French restaurant during his second weekend in New York.

"I don't know," responded Beverly.

"How does having three children, built-in, feel to you?"

"I don't know. I don't know little children."

"I want you to think about whether you could marry me," he said.

Nothing more was ever spoken on the subject. As far as Peter was concerned, the whole matter was settled. They celebrated New Year's Eve at Tordo's restaurant in Hartsdale, New York. After dinner, Peter reached for his customary Cuban cigar. "It's me or the cigar," Beverly teased.

He chose Beverly. "He began drinking toasts to the happy life we were going to have. It was a *fait accompli,*" she says.

While the couple's future together was never in question, the size of the diamond in Beverly's engagement ring was. Whenever Peter would board a plane for Cleveland, it was a running joke between them that he would hold up two fingers for two carats, and Beverly would hold up three. In February 1956, Peter surprised her with a three-carat diamond ring.

"My mother wanted us to wait six weeks after the divorce so that if I became pregnant early it wouldn't look as if he had to marry me," says Beverly.

Mother prevailed. Peter's divorce came through at the end of September. On November 17, 1956, two weeks after the close of the City Opera season, the lovers were married by a state Supreme Court justice in the studio of Beverly's voice coach, Estelle Liebling. Beverly wore a pearl wreath in her hair and a short white wedding dress that her mother had fashioned from a beautiful piece of antique lace. Beverly's mother, Shirley, who sewed all of Beverly's costumes, designed the trousseau. Only family members and a handful of friends attended the ceremony and the luncheon that followed at Hampshire House in New York.

The couple spent their honeymoon on Nassau, where Peter had rented a villa at the Balmoral Club and chartered Errol Flynn's yacht.

As time passed, the couple's running joke about the size of Beverly's diamond engagement ring endured. Several years later, Peter bought Beverly another diamond worthy of all the fingers on both hands — ten carats. Together, they had a son, Peter Jr., and daughter, Meredith. The family lived in Cleveland until 1960, when they moved to Boston, and later put down roots in New York.

Joanne Woodward and Paul Newman

Married January 29, 1958

It was 1952 and a hot August day in New York when Joanne Woodward first met Paul Newman at the office of their mutual agent, Maynard Morris. She was sticky and uncomfortable from the heat. He looked cool and neat in his seersucker suit. "I disliked him intensely on first sight," she remembers. "I thought he was too pretty for words."

Fortunately, their professional paths soon crossed again. Paul was cast in a supporting role in *Picnic* on Broadway. Joanne was hired as an understudy for the two female leads, Janice Rule and Kim Stanley. The play won a Pulitzer Prize for William Inge and ran fourteen months, and Joanne and Paul, both intensely committed to their careers, became backstage friends. Paul, who grew up in Cleveland, was twenty-seven, married and six months out of Yale Drama School. Joanne, twenty-two, from Thomasville, Georgia, had already put in two years in New York. "We were all very close in that play, because it was a first play for almost everyone," Joanne explains.

With plenty of work available on stage and in live television dramas, it was an electrifying time to be a talented young New York actor. Still, there wasn't much going on in summer, so like so many others, Joanne and Paul headed for California. "Of course, we all stuck together because there was a great cachet in those days in being a New York actor. It was a form of snobbism that one kept one's New York status," recalls Joanne.

Paul had been married since age twenty-four and was the father of three small children. Joanne had been too focused on her career to think about marriage and family. "The only person who was interested in me getting married was my mother," she says. "She was very nervous about my being an old maid. I don't think I ever seriously thought about marrying anybody; they may have thought about marrying me, but I didn't think about marrying them."

Though gossip columnists at the time breathlessly reported Joanne's engagements – including one to novelist/playwright Gore Vidal and another to playwright James Costigan – she says none of it was true. "Oh, my heavens, no! Costi and Gore were my best friends."

By 1957, Paul and his wife, who had remained in New York with their children, separated. While he and Joanne were working together in *The Long Hot Summer,* their feelings for one another deepened. "We were together from the time we did *Long Hot Summer.* That was it," she says. They were a couple.

"We were friends for a very long time, and there wasn't a courting stage. We went past that. We knew each other too well. It's always a good idea to be friends first. In this day and age, it's all very free sex and all of that, and it seems to me, the cart comes before the horse."

When the couple was together, they usually went to the movies – Joanne and Paul could watch movies all day and all night. "They weren't like dates," says Joanne. "It was either the two of us or we had very good friends who were with us all the time. If we did have a date, sometimes it would be me and Paul and Gore or five of us or six of us."

The Long Hot Summer wrapped in November, and by January they planned to get married. Joanne's biological clock was ticking. "I was twenty-eight and I suddenly thought: Well, wait a minute, maybe it is time." Paul wasn't the type to get down on his hands and knees. She laughingly calls it his "un-proposal." "It would have been nice to have had some romantic thing we could have told our children. But Paul's not traditionally romantic. He has a sense of humor about it. He literally did decide in a week. We had time to get married and go on a honeymoon to Europe for two weeks before he had to start *Cat on a Hot Tin Roof.*"

Within one week, Paul flew south for a Mexican divorce. Joanne discussed their imminent nuptials with Edward R. Murrow on his TV show *Person to Person* and the newsman urged the newlyweds to stay at the quintessentially British Connaught Hotel in London. The couple met up in Las Vegas on January 29, 1958, for a civil ceremony at El Rancho Vegas. A few friends and business associates joined them. Not even their families had enough notice to be there.

Though Paul gave Joanne a small diamond necklace, there was no time to pick out rings. "What are we going to get married with?" a nervous Joanne asked her intended.

"Don't worry about it. I'll find something," he answered.

What he found was a cheap silver band. "It was the strangest looking thing I ever saw in my life," she says.

Paul wore a dark suit; Joanne, a short ivory faille dress and matching jacket that she had custom-made at Jax in Beverly Hills "in nothing flat." "It was not the most romantic thing I've ever seen," she admits. "Someone got the room and someone got the cake. At the wedding, of all people, was Eydie Gorme, whom I didn't know, but she happened to be playing in Vegas."

After watching Joe E. Lewis' show, the couple caught a flight to New York. The next night, Joanne's father and stepmother gave a party for all the relatives. The following day, Joanne and Paul left for a holiday in France, Switzerland and England, where they followed Murrow's advice and stayed at the Connaught.

In London's Burlington Arcade, Paul bought Joanne an antique wedding ring with several small diamonds and the initial "J" on the underside. They added an "N."

The couple had three children over the years and continued to make movies together. In 1968, Paul made his debut behind the camera, directing his wife in *Rachel, Rachel,* for which she was nominated for an Academy Award. On their tenth anniversary, he gave her a plain white-gold wedding band. On their twenty-fifth, he gave her a yellow diamond band. They miscalculated and missed their thirty-fifth anniversary, though Paul promised to give Joanne another piece of jewelry on their fortieth.

Alma Johnson and Colin Powell

Married August 24, 1962

The same qualities that served one of America's most famous soldiers during war — assertiveness, bravery, fearlessness — were also evident during his maneuvers to win the heart of the woman he loved. In November, 1961, Colin Powell was on his way to becoming a nationally recognized hero, the youngest and the first African-American chairman of the United States Joint Chiefs of Staff and leader of Operation Desert Storm during the Persian Gulf War. However, when they met, Alma Johnson wasn't easily won over.

She was an audiologist at the Boston Guild for the Hard of Hearing when her roommate, Jacqueline Fields, pressured her into a date with a young man who had just been promoted to a captain in the U.S. Army and was serving in the Fifth Infantry Division at Fort Devens, Massachusetts.

"I don't go on blind dates, and I definitely don't go out with soldiers," Alma told Jacqueline. But Jacqueline insisted. After all, Alma was twenty-four and single, and Colin, twenty-five, was such a nice person.

There were no fireworks on their first date at a Boston nightclub, but both Colin and Alma had a pleasant evening. Alma, with her warm smile, possessed a quiet strength and intelligence. Colin was a man of few words, but Alma could see his virtues. He asked her out for the following weekend, and the following, and the following. It became routine: Alma would take the bus to Fort Devens on Friday nights, and Colin would drive her home on Sundays.

Many of their dates were at the officers' club with married couples, and Alma enjoyed the camaraderie of army life. But deep down, she didn't understand Colin's choice of a military career. She had never before met a man who had joined the army by choice.

Colin invited her to his parents' New Year's Eve party in the South Bronx, New

York. "Maybe I will," she said coyly, before deciding to go.

Colin came from a tight-knit family. His parents were immigrants from Jamaica and hoped that Colin would eventually marry a Jamaican girl. They socialized with other Jamaicans and held certain prejudices against southern blacks. Alma was from Birmingham, Alabama, and her father wasn't thrilled about her marrying a Jamaican, whom he didn't even meet until just before the wedding.

After the new year, the couple began to see each other exclusively. Colin was now picking her up and driving her to New York for the weekend to spend time with his family and friends, who welcomed her once they assessed the seriousness of the relationship. Two events may have prompted Colin's decision to propose in August. The first was a phone call from Ronnie Brooks, one of his closest friends from his Reserve Officer Training Corps days, who told Colin that he had heard about a special girl he wanted to meet named Alma Johnson. "Forget it, I already did," Colin told him.

The second occurrence was orders to leave immediately for a one-year tour of duty in Vietnam. When Colin told Alma, she didn't offer to wait for him.

"I don't want to tell you I'll be here when you get back," she said firmly. "I'm too old for that. I may write, I may not. But I don't really want to go through all of that." A week later, Colin gathered his nerve. "Okay, this is what we are going to do," he told her. "We'll get married in two weeks. You'll go home next week to get ready for the wedding, I'll come down the week after that, and we'll get married."

Those were the orders Alma was waiting to hear.

They married on August 24, 1962, at her parents' home in Birmingham. Also present was Colin's family and his best man, Ronnie Brooks.

Four months later, while Alma was pregnant, Colin went to Vietnam, where he led a combat unit near the North Vietnamese border. Their son, Michael, was three weeks old when Colin heard the news about the birth. The couple also has two daughters, Linda and Annemarie.

"*As an army wife, never forget that you are the 'silent' member of the team, but, nonetheless, a key 'man'.*"
— *from a book given to brides before military weddings*

Sophia Loren and Carlo Ponti

Married April 9, 1966

As a child in Pozzuoli, Italy, Sophia Loren saw a wedding in the village church. The bride wore a beautiful white gown and carried a bouquet of orange blossoms, and two children held her veil. It was during World War II, when bombs were falling and every day was a struggle. "At that moment, the world stopped for me," she remembers. "I was almost paralyzed with enchantment. I am still convinced I actually heard angels' harps anticipating Mendelssohn's nuptial march of the organ."

That vision haunted and eluded Sophia for decades. "Life didn't want such a dream of mine to come true," she says. Her own trip to the altar was a long and troubled one. But goaded on by competition from Cary Grant, her great love, Carlo Ponti, eventually did wed the star he helped create.

They met in 1950. Sofia Scicolone, then going by the name Sofia Lazzaro, was sixteen years old, shy, unsophisticated, a poor country girl who had come to Rome that year at the urging of her mother to try to break into movies. She reluctantly participated in a "Miss Rome" contest, for which successful movie producer Carlo Ponti, thirty-seven, was a judge. Carlo had launched the careers of numerous actresses, including the great Italian star Gina Lollobrigida. Not surprisingly, at the contest he saw something magical in the voluptuous young girl who placed second.

Two years later, Carlo was managing Sophia's career, even sending her some money occasionally to sustain her. Carlo was married with two children, but he was undeniably attracted to the strong-willed, stunning young actress. Sophia saw Carlo as more than a trusted advisor and friend; he was also something of a father figure – her own father had abandoned her mother before Sophia was born. They began to see each other secretly, although she, a strict Catholic, wouldn't consummate their relationship.

In 1954, she was cast in Vittorio de Sica's *Gold of Naples* and her career shifted to an entirely different level. So did her relationship with Carlo. On the set of her next film, he presented her with a small diamond ring. Carlo, never a man for speeches, said not a word about the ring's significance. But to her it was a symbol of his seriousness. She was ready to give herself to him completely now, even though he was still living with his wife, Giuliana, and had no plans to leave her.

Then, in 1957, another suitor entered the equation. Sophia was cast opposite Frank Sinatra and Cary Grant in a drama filmed in Spain, *The Pride and the Passion.* She and Cary quickly fell in love – but she also still loved Carlo. On location, Cary, who was still married to his third wife, actress Betsy Drake, told Sophia he wanted to marry her. She told him she needed time.

Since divorce wasn't recognized in Italy, Carlo was now moved to make what Sophia recalls as a somewhat feeble attempt at an annulment on the grounds that when he was married he didn't believe in the sacrament of marriage. The Vatican denied the annulment, but Carlo left his wife. By now, Sophia and Carlo were in Hollywood where she was making *Houseboat* with Cary, who was still pursuing her.

It was at this point that Sophia decided that she had waited long enough for Carlo. Well aware that Cary's frequent phone calls to the bungalow at the Bel-Air Hotel that she shared with Carlo provided not-so-subtle leverage in her behalf, she delivered her ultimatum. She wanted a life of her own, children and a wedding band, she told Carlo. It was now up to him to make a decision.

Looking back at that time, Sophia says: "After so many years, having gone through so many good and less good events, happy mother of two grown-up boys, I still vividly remember those short, tense moments when I asked all that of Carlo. All my fears, my dreams, my career were right there, thrown like dice on a blackjack table. But still, I had to wait a few agonizing days before I had his first firm answer and concrete action."

The action came when *Houseboat* was just wrapping up. Carlo and Sophia were eating breakfast at the hotel when Carlo handed her a newspaper folded open to Louella Parsons' column. The lead item read that Carlo had obtained a Mexican divorce and married Sophia by proxy in the same courtroom on September 17, 1957. At last, a wedding, even if neither of them was present. She was overjoyed. Carlo gave her a wedding band, and that night the couple dined and celebrated alone in their bungalow.

Less than a month passed, however, before the Pontis' nuptial bliss was shattered. The Catholic Church would not recognize the marriage: Carlo was legally charged with bigamy, with Sophia named as his *"concubina,"* and they were unable to return to Rome as husband and wife. Other Italians had obtained Mexican divorces before, but Sophia and Carlo apparently were forced to be an example.

Carlo and Sophia went home anyway, but to avoid arrest, began living under assumed names, moving frequently and never appearing together in public. They explored all possible legal measures, but couldn't find a way out of their nightmare until 1966, when Giuliana, Carlo's wife, came up with a plan. Carlo, Sophia and Giuliana all moved to France and each applied for French citizenship. Then Carlo and Giuliana obtained a legal French divorce.

Sophia and Carlo were finally married on April 9, 1966. It was not until that simple, morning ceremony in the city hall of Sèvres, outside Paris, that Sophia heard her long-awaited harps playing. "The bare walls of the room were glittering like a Bengal firework," she recalls. "I knew that Carlo, although unaware of my childish vision, was in some way sharing it. The room in Sèvres suddenly was an immense cathedral to me, and we were leaving behind all the difficulties and unbearable anxieties of the past."

In 1968 their first son, Carlo Jr., was born. His brother, Edoardo, followed in 1973.

Dolly Parton and Carl Dean

Married May 30, 1966

One day in the summer of 1964, Carl Dean, age twenty-one, was cruising through Nashville on the lookout for pretty girls. And there was no ignoring eighteen-year-old Dolly Parton, barely five-foot-one with Mae West curves, as she strolled through downtown on her first day in the country-music capital.

The fourth of twelve children born to a poor farmer in the Great Smoky Mountains of Tennessee, Dolly was the first person in her family to graduate from high school. Music was already her life by then: she'd been writing songs since she was five and appeared at the Grand Ole Opry at twelve. Now she'd set her sights on Nashville, ready to seek her fame and fortune as a singer and songwriter.

While her clothes ran through the wash cycle at the Wishy Washy Laundry, Dolly was taking in the neighborhood sights when an attractive man in a white Chevy Impala waved her down. Carl, who was born and raised in Nashville and worked with his father in the asphalt paving business, had never seen anyone like Dolly before. And she was a sight to behold in her hip huggers and ruffled crop top. To his good fortune, she waved right back, since friendly gestures came naturally to people from Sevier County.

Meeting men always came easily to Dolly. "I was a flirt – and I still am!" she admits. "I'm like Will Rogers. I never met a man I didn't like."

Carl made a U-turn, pulled up to the curb and struck up a conversation. To Dolly's surprise, he followed her inside the laundromat to lend a hand folding her clothes. Dolly, who had two boyfriends back home, turned down Carl's request for a date. After he persisted, she permitted him to visit her the next day at her baby-sitting job, one of several chores the determined and hard-working young woman already had taken on to pay the rent.

Carl stopped by to see her every day at work that week, and then he tried asking her out again. This time she accepted, and he took her to his parents' house for dinner. "Fix this girl a plate, she's the girl I'm gonna marry," Carl announced to everyone's astonishment. Dolly, who had been like a mother to her younger siblings and never had any desire to marry, thought he must be kidding. Carl, however, was serious.

He never made any mention of love or marriage after that, but she kept on seeing him when she wasn't out of town performing at small nightclubs. Besides being tall (six-foot-three), well-built and handsome, with dark hair and eyes, Carl was, she thought, sensible and down-to-earth. He was his own man, that was for sure. He just wasn't the type to make formal dates. More likely, he'd just show up at Dolly's whenever he felt like it.

Over the next two years, Dolly was so busy pounding the streets that she didn't worry too much about Carl's romantic strategy – or lack of one. During that time, Carl went to boot camp for the Army Reserve and was "building up his nerve" to propose, says Dolly. Finally, when she moved in the opposite direction from Carl's house, he notified her one night during one of his surprise visits, "You're gonna have to move to the other side of town or we're gonna have to get married."

"Are you proposing, is that an ultimatum or what?" she said.

"No, I'm serious, move or marry me," he said.

"Well, you've never even said you love me," said Dolly.

"Hell, you know I love you."

By now, Dolly had a recording contract, and her producer didn't think marriage would fit in with her plans to become a star. As for Carl, he had an inkling that Dolly's ambitions would take her on the road and away from home, but since he adored her and wanted her to be happy, he believed they should be married as soon as possible. So to keep the news away from her producer and avoid attention from newspaper reporters, the couple decided to be married in secret.

In April 1966, Dolly took Carl home to meet her family. The next month, on May 30, 1966 – Memorial Day – they were married by Reverend Don Duvall at the First Baptist Church in Ringold, Georgia – they went to Georgia simply to keep reports of their marriage out of the Nashville papers. Dolly wore a short white dress and veil and Carl wore a dark suit. "We bought a small set of rings at Sears with Carl's mother's credit card. We both paid on it for many years." She still wears the simple diamond engagement ring and wedding band.

There was "no party, no champagne, no cake," she recalls. "My mother cooked dinner in Nashville and went to Georgia with us for the wedding."

As they were driving back to Nashville, Dolly's mother, Avie Lee, discovered she had left her purse in the church, so they had to turn around again to retrieve it, a trip that used up most of the couple's one-day honeymoon before they had to return to work the next day.

The average cost of photography at a wedding is one thousand dollars, less than ten percent of the total nuptial budget.

Priscilla Beaulieu and Elvis Presley

Married May 1, 1967

From the time she moved to Memphis at age seventeen to finish high school near Elvis Presley, Priscilla Beaulieu knew they would marry someday. "The mystery was *when*," she remembers. "That was Elvis' way of keeping the romance alive."

Priscilla was aware that other women before her had used pressure tactics to no avail, so marriage was a topic she rarely brought up. She didn't need to. There were signs here and there. "He talked a lot about children, and we imagined what they would look like and what they would do," says Priscilla. And there were his many gifts. "This is nothing," Elvis would say upon presenting her with a bauble. "Just wait."

At that time, Priscilla was in no rush to marry. She had her own room at Graceland and was happy with the relationship just as it was. "It was going well. We were doing so much, traveling back and forth to California. Some friends of ours, especially in Hollywood, were breaking up and that scared both of us."

Besides, the cameo beauty was only fourteen when they met during Elvis' famed tour of duty in Wiesbaden, West Germany, in 1959. There had been times at first when the ten years between them seemed insurmountable. At twenty-four, Elvis was already a legend, and he was naturally confused about his feelings for the ninth-grade student living overseas with her mother and Air Force captain stepfather. "We had a very romantic relationship," says Priscilla, "but Elvis was always conscious of the age difference. He didn't want 'jail bait' to dampen his image, and he was protective of throwing me to the media. He also knew he would be leaving Germany and didn't want to hurt me."

Before he returned to the United States, six months after their meeting, Elvis told Priscilla he loved her, but still he wasn't sure how to proceed. Even though he had a girlfriend in Memphis, he wrote and telephoned the love-struck Priscilla often. Their conversations, she remembers, frequently lasted for several hours.

During the following two years, Elvis invited Priscilla for occasional visits – Christmases at Graceland, a trip to Las Vegas and another to Los Angeles. They were always chaperoned by Elvis' friends and family members. In 1962, Elvis came up with the novel idea for Priscilla to finish her high school education in Memphis, and phoned her stepfather, Captain Paul Beaulieu, for his permission. He assured the Beaulieus that Priscilla would live at his father Vernon's house, attend a good school and always be chaperoned, and implied that he would marry her when she came of age. He must have been a sweet talker. Reluctantly, her parents approved. Vernon enrolled Priscilla at Immaculate Conception, a girls' school in Memphis, while Elvis was in Los Angeles filming *Fun in Acapulco.*

Unbeknownst to her family, bit by bit she moved from Vernon's house into Elvis' mansion. The couple often stayed up all night with Elvis' entourage, and Priscilla would sleepwalk through her classes the following day. After graduating, she continued to live with Elvis at Graceland and at his house in Bel-Air for four more years, molding herself to Elvis' lifestyle, one that she loved but that was hardly typical for a teenager.

One day, for no apparent reason, Elvis presented her with a three-sapphire-and-diamond ring, which he had worn himself for years. Priscilla knew it was symbolic. "He loved it and wore it all the time. I knew it meant a lot to him. It solidified the relationship."

Late one December evening in 1966, Elvis knocked on her bedroom door. "I was in my dressing room getting ready to go to a movie," she says, alluding to one of their nightly treks to the Memphian Theater, which Elvis rented after closing time.

Priscilla playfully asked for his password. "Fire Eyes," he responded, using her nickname for him.

When he entered, she wondered what he was holding behind his back. "He had a jeweler come to the house earlier that evening, but I hadn't associated it with a proposal," Priscilla recalls. "It was Christmas, and he was buying gifts for his family. It was a common thing."

"I have a surprise," Elvis told her. He got down on his knees and handed her a box. Inside was an engagement ring – a three-and-a-half-carat diamond surrounded by a detachable row of smaller diamonds.

Elvis, very much in command most times, became shy and nervous. Although he was announcing his decision rather than asking her to marry him, he said it in their own private language, speaking partly in the third person.

"We're going to be married," said Elvis. "You're going to be his. I told you I'd know when the time was right. Well, the time's right."

"I was awestruck at first because I had no idea," says Priscilla. "I had tears in my eyes, and he in his. I cried. I didn't expect it. I threw my arms around him, and we held each other." Still in each other's embrace, they excitedly went downstairs to share the news and show the ring to his family. Then, just like any other night, every-one went off together to a midnight movie, where Elvis made the announcement to his friends.

"Colonel" Tom Parker, who managed Elvis' career, planned a private wedding at the Aladdin Hotel in Las Vegas. A justice of the Nevada Supreme Court married the couple at 9:41 a.m. on May 1, 1967. About a dozen family members and friends watched as Priscilla, twenty-one, wearing a long, empire-style white gown and tulle veil, and Elvis, thirty-two, wearing a tuxedo, exchanged vows. After the ceremony, the Presleys flew on Frank Sinatra's Learjet, the *Christina,* to their rented house in Palm Springs. Elvis sang "The Hawaiian Wedding Song" as he carried Priscilla across the threshold. Four weeks later, they put on their wedding clothes again and hosted a wedding reception for sixty guests at Graceland.

On February 1, 1968, their daughter, Lisa Marie, was born. The marriage ended in divorce six years later. Elvis died at Graceland on August 16, 1977.

Shakira Baksh and Michael Caine

Married January 8, 1973

Ever since he became a major international film star with his breakthrough title role as the indefatigable Cockney womanizer in *Alfie,* Michael Caine was in the enviable position of having his pick of women. Still, there was one desirable female who was hardly falling at his feet.

Michael – thirty-eight-years old and loaded with charm – was not one to spend time in his London flat watching television, but one evening, in the spring of 1971, he cooked up some of his favorite boyhood Cockney fry-up for dinner and settled in with the telly. He says he fell madly in love the moment he saw the gorgeous, dark-haired Brazilian girl shaking maracas in a Maxwell House coffee commercial. He intended to fly to Brazil the next day to find her.

Later that night, when Michael went off to a discotheque and mentioned the girl to a friend, he learned that he could save himself a trip. His friend knew the star of the commercial – Shakira Baksh – and she wasn't Brazilian. The stunning model in her early twenties was born in Guyana and was crowned Miss Guyana in the 1967 Miss World contest. She had been living in London ever since. Their mutual friend, after checking with Shakira the next day, provided Michael with her phone number.

Michael called immediately, asking to see her that night, but his reputation as a rogue, once divorced with a daughter, had preceded him. Shakira had already met her share of playboys. "I knew a lot about him – he was a womanizer. He was hot stuff," she explains. "My flat mates all said, 'Don't do this!' "

Shakira told Michael she was busy every night that week, but gave him permission to call again the following week. Precisely one week later, Michael called again, and she agreed to see him. On their first date, Shakira kept up her guard and wouldn't allow him in her flat. But to Michael, meeting her was the single most thrilling moment of his life. Overwhelmed by her beauty and refined manner, he made up his

· 9 9 ·

mind on that day to spend the rest of his life with her.

Four months later, Shakira moved in with Michael, even though she was still concerned about his reputation and was uncertain about the chances of a lasting relationship. She decided she'd give the relationship six months. Over the next year, she realized that the relationship would last. Michael started to refer to her as his wife, even though they never officially discussed marriage.

A year and a half after they met, Shakira learned unexpectedly that she was pregnant. She shared the news with Michael when they were seated in the back of his chauffeur-driven Rolls-Royce en route to his country house in Windsor.

"Will you marry me then?" Caine immediately responded. She began to cry. "It was so sweet the way he did it," she says. "Michael can be a rebellious little boy, but he has a very tender side."

Because he was in the middle of filming *Sleuth,* the couple had to wait three months to marry. Since they wanted a small, private wedding that wouldn't attract the attention of the press, they decided to tie the knot in Las Vegas, Nevada. On January 8, 1973, they gathered at the Candlelight Wedding Chapel accompanied by Caine's agent and his publicist. Shakira wore a long white dress she had purchased that morning at Saks Fifth Avenue in Beverly Hills. After the ceremony, the Caines flew back to Los Angeles and spent the night in the Beverly Wilshire Hotel's honeymoon suite. A few days later their Hollywood friends gave them a grand wedding party. Their daughter, Natasha, was born six months later.

In 1972, ten percent of adults lived with an unmarried mate before their first marriage. In 1992, almost fifty percent did.

Hillary Rodham and Bill Clinton

Married October 11, 1975

Bill Clinton first eyed Hillary Rodham in a class on civil liberties at Yale Law School in 1970. There were only about seventy-five women among the some five hundred students admitted that year to the law school, and Hillary, remarkably self-assured and driven, stood out even among the *crème de la crème*.

For that matter, so did Bill. Hillary noticed him first in the student lounge. As she walked past, she overheard him boasting, in his Southern lilt, that in the state of Arkansas, "... we have the biggest watermelons in the world." Since conversations in the Yale student lounge tended to be more cerebral, Hillary wondered aloud to a friend, "Who is that?"

"That's Bill Clinton from Arkansas, and *that* [Arkansas] is all he ever talks about," said her friend.

The two just couldn't seem to ignore each other. Bill was handsome, with an easy-going charm and a boyish smile that could make grown women wilt. Hillary, twenty-three, even in her *au naturel* state – no makeup, Coke-bottle eyeglasses, flannel shirts and untended brown hair – also had a definite magnetism.

When Hillary caught Bill staring at her again, this time in the law school library, she decided to make the first move. She got up from her chair and marched right over. "If you're going to keep looking at me and I'm going to keep looking at you, we ought to at least know each other. I'm Hillary Rodham."

Stunned by her boldness, Bill, twenty-four, later recalled: "I couldn't remember my name."

"I knew from the minute I saw her that if I got involved with her I would fall in love with her," Bill told *Newsweek* magazine years later.

Their first date was strictly casual, a stroll through a Yale art gallery during a

Mark Rothko exhibit. Though they had vastly different upbringings, they discovered that they saw the world through remarkably similar eyes. Hillary had transformed from a sash-wearing "Goldwater Girl" in Park Ridge, a conservative, middle-class suburb of Chicago, to a liberal political activist and president of the student government at Wellesley. A political science major, she was a natural-born organizer and student leader involved in rallies for everything from improved minority admissions to banning curfews. She was the first student invited to deliver a commencement address (which she did without notes), an accomplishment that landed her picture in *Life* magazine.

Bill, who grew up in the rural outposts of Hope and, later, Hot Springs, Arkansas, had been intent on a career in medicine until, at the age of sixteen, he shook hands with President John F. Kennedy in the White House Rose Garden. From that point on, he thought only of politics. While enrolled at Georgetown University, he spent his junior year working for Senator William J. Fulbright of Arkansas, then chairman of the Senate Foreign Relations Committee. After graduating in 1969, he attended Oxford as a Rhodes scholar. In 1970, he enrolled at Yale, a year after Hillary.

It was a perfect match. Both were both kind of square. Neither had their sights set on a high-paying law career. Instead, both saw their futures centered around public service. Everyone knew that Bill was planning to run for public office. Hillary was already absorbed in children's rights and planned to spend the summer working for the Children's Defense Fund.

Not everyone, however, thought that they were made for each other. "You should stick to Southern girls," his mother, Virginia Kelley, and brother Roger both informed Bill after they came to New Haven to watch Bill and Hillary in moot court.

A year after they met, they were living together in a rented house. Graduating a year ahead of Bill, Hillary decided to stay with him in New Haven and study child development at the Yale Child Study Center.

After he graduated, Bill took a job teaching at the University of Arkansas Law School in Fayetteville. Hillary went to work as an attorney at the Children's Defense Fund until she became a counsel for the House Judiciary Committee impeachment investigation of President Richard Nixon.

While they were apart, they racked up hefty phone bills talking late into the night. When Nixon resigned, Hillary disregarded offers from top law firms in New York, Chicago and Washington, D.C., and made her move to Fayetteville. She was going to try it there for a year. "I loved him," she explained. "I had to."

Bill was absorbed in his ill-fated run for Congress, and Hillary started teaching criminal law and trial advocacy at the University of Arkansas and founded the school's legal aid program. She went back home to think things over. When she returned, Bill picked her up at the airport.

"I bought that house you like, so you better marry me because I can't live in it by myself," he announced.

Their brick house was the setting for their wedding on October 11, 1975. Hillary, Bill and their families stayed up half the night painting it. Bill wanted a big bash, and Hillary had something more intimate in mind. They compromised on a private ceremony followed by a reception for one hundred at the home of state Democratic Party chairman Morris Henry and his wife, Ann. Hillary wore an old-fashioned-looking dress designed by Jessica McClintock, which she bought in a hurry at Dillard's department store. For the occasion, she left her eyeglasses off. The wedding cake was iced with pale yellow roses.

They honeymooned in Acapulco. A year later, Bill was elected Arkansas State Attorney General and they moved to Little Rock. In 1978, he became the country's youngest governor but was defeated in his re-election bid two years later. Hillary kept her maiden name as First Lady of Arkansas, but public sentiment forced her to adopt Bill's surname before his successful 1982 gubernatorial campaign. In 1980, their daughter, Chelsea, was born. Bill was elected President of the United States in 1992. Hillary, once named by the *National Law Review* as one of the "100 Most Influential Lawyers in America," became known as Bill's presidential partner as well as First Lady.

Diandra Luker and Michael Douglas

Married March 20, 1977

It took an independent and strong-minded woman who wasn't impressed with his father's name or with his own status as one of Hollywood's leading heartthrobs to make Michael Douglas think of settling down within a few weeks of their first meeting.

Michael was thirty-two when he was in Washington, D.C., with bachelor buddies Warren Beatty and Jack Nicholson for the parties surrounding Jimmy Carter's presidential inauguration in 1977. Standing at an hors d'oeuvres table during one such event, he spotted a Renaissance beauty with delicate features and cascading gold hair.

Michael's fame as the stud detective on the television police series *The Streets of San Francisco* didn't carry any weight with Diandra Luker. Television sets were absent from the home where she grew up on the island of Majorca, off the coast of Spain, and at her boarding school in Switzerland.

Diandra spoke five languages and was planning a career following in the footsteps of her U.S. diplomat-father, who died when she was a child. At the time, she was working as a White House intern while enrolled as a freshman at Georgetown University's School of Foreign Service.

"I recognized Jack, and everyone was saying who Warren was. I thought, 'Oh, this is trouble,' " she recalls. "I grew up in Europe where people thought the movie business was not something to aspire to. Back then, that was the way it was."

Michael, whose eyes were following her from canape to canape, sported a thick beard and long hair from his just-completed part in *The China Syndrome*. Diandra might have dismissed him as another Hollywood roué, but because of his Bohemian demeanor she presumed he must be a painter or a writer. That probability intrigued her, she admits.

Nevertheless, she shot down Michael's opening line – "Would you like some mustard?" – with a curt, "No, thank you." He persisted with offers of other food items along the buffet long enough to spark a conversation. Soon after, when Diandra and her friends left to go to a members-only nightclub, Pisces, Michael attempted to tag along. Diandra tried to discourage him, telling him he'd never get in.

"No problem, they'll let me in," Michael said assuredly. He dumped Jack and Warren and headed to Pisces.

Snubbed at the door, Michael worried that he might never see Diandra again. "It was a magical evening from the beginning," he recalls, "Jimmy Carter's inauguration, amongst good friends and seeing a real-life angel for the first time. That's the only way I could describe Diandra. She looked like an angel from another century."

Michael's cab driver gave him a quarter and suggested he call her at the club from a phone booth: "It's me. You're right. They won't let me in," he told Diandra.

Now that he had her on the phone, Michael thought he'd impress her with an invitation to the Inauguration the next day. Diandra accepted. But his seats proved to be so far away, and the January weather so frigid, that the two left and went to lunch.

As they warmed up, Diandra's frosty demeanor started to melt away too. "Then we fell madly in love," she says. "I think it started at the hors d'oeuvres table. He had very beautiful green eyes. I thought he was different and extremely bright. He doesn't read Freud all day, but he has an innate astuteness about life. I still had this romantic notion that he was a painter and not part of the diplomatic, political world I knew so well."

Michael spent the rest of the week in Washington. It wasn't until about their fourth date that she learned his true profession. "It was too late," she said. "I was already in love."

Michael liked the idea that Diandra wasn't easily impressed with Hollywood or that he was the son of Kirk Douglas. Diandra was not only on the bookish side, she wasn't eager to ride in Hollywood's fast lane.

Michael returned to Los Angeles determined to see her again. "Diandra has the most attractive combination of intellect and humor – two qualities that can go a long way," says Michael. "Combining those with her international and multilingual background creates an extraordinary union. I also felt that she was wise beyond her years in certain areas and a lovely woman/child in others."

He called every day. By the end of the week, he invited her to spend the weekend in southern California.

"I told my roommate, 'If my mother calls, tell her I'm at the library,' " Diandra remembers.

Diandra's weekend, lodged in Michael's apartment on La Cienega Boulevard, stretched into one week, then two. "I don't think your mother believes me," Diandra's roommate warned her about the library ruse. Diandra and Michael now discussed the possibility of his moving to Washington or her moving to California. At that point, they decided that geography wasn't going to keep them apart.

They were driving back from a warm and approving meeting with his mother, Diane, when Michael turned to Diandra and said simply, "I think we should get married. Will you marry me? I love you and can't live without you."

"I know it sounds strange, but we just knew that was the way it was going to be almost immediately," says Diandra.

While Michael's father, Kirk, and stepmother, Anne, also gave their blessing to the pair, Diandra recalls that her mother, Patricia de Morrell, suspicious that Diandra seemed to have moved into the library, flew to Washington to see what was going on. Her mother was "absolutely furious" about her deception, Diandra says, and summoned her back to school. Diandra stayed long enough to take midterm exams before flying back to Los Angeles for good. Diandra made it clear to Michael, though, that she had every intention of finishing her education and getting a job.

They were married two months after they met at the hors d'oeuvres table, on March 20, 1977, in a garden wedding before two hundred guests at the home of Michael's father and stepmother. A dinner reception for five hundred followed at the Beverly Wilshire Hotel. Diandra wore a knee-length, white silk wedding dress she had designed with a friend, and her large, round diamond solitaire engagement ring. Michael wore a three-piece suit. They sealed their union with a diamond wedding band and honeymooned in Palm Springs.

Diandra graduated from the University of California at Santa Barbara, ran the office of film and television at the Metropolitan Museum in New York and produces documentary and art films. Their son, Cameron, was born a year after they were married.

Norris Church and Norman Mailer

Married November 11, 1980

When Norman Mailer was introduced to Norris Church at a party in Arkansas in April 1975, he was so awed by her beauty that he was rendered speechless and walked away.

"Oh, my gosh, he must hate tall women," thought the statuesque Norris, twenty-six, who had once been a member of the homecoming queen's court at Atkins High in Atkins, Arkansas.

Then a high school art teacher in Russellville, Arkansas, Norris had written a novel herself and was entrenched in the town's literary circle. Since she had just finished reading Norman's biography of Marilyn Monroe, Norris jumped at the chance to meet the famous author, journalist and essayist from New York.

Norman, fifty-two, would stop off to see his World War II buddy Francis Gwaltney, a professor at Arkansas Tech, whenever his travels took him south. Norman spoke to Francis' class the same day that Norris happened to be on campus with her art students. When she heard that Norman was going to be a guest at a cocktail party at her former college professor's house that evening, she called Francis and inquired, "Can I crash?"

Five-foot-ten in her bare feet, Norris arrived at the party in jeans, a shirt tied at the midriff and platform sandals. She not only stood out in a crowd of buttoned-up professors, she towered over practically everyone, including the five-foot-seven man of letters.

"It was a funny meeting," she recalls. "Norman walked across the room, said, 'How do you do,' shook hands and turned around and walked out of the room."

A little while later, Francis invited Norris to join a small group that included Norman for dinner.

"I think that's a bad idea," said Norris. "I don't think Norman liked me very much."

"*Like* you? – it was *his* idea," said Francis.

There was a lot of flirting that night between the much-married writer and the once-divorced school teacher who soon discovered they were born a minute apart on January 31. The dinner took place at another friend's house out in the woods. Norman and Norris stood on the porch overlooking a brook and talked half the evening. "It was a magical night," Norris says.

Both agree they fell in love that night. "Besides the chemistry, I was then and still am fascinated with his mind. He never ceases to amuse me and amaze me and enter-tain me. And I love the twinkle in his blue eyes," she adds.

Norris was unlike anyone who traveled in Norman's circle. After graduating from Harvard and serving in the Army, the Jewish boy from Brooklyn wrote his war novel *The Naked and the Dead* and became an instant star and *enfant terrible* of the liter-ary establishment. Norris was a model of small-town normalcy, whose tranquil center came from a strict Freewill Baptist upbringing and an extremely close family life. As she says, "Norman never encountered a fundamental Baptist before. His curiosity was endless."

The next morning, Norman left for New York but returned to Russellville two weeks later. Norris joined him in Chicago during his book tour for *The Fight.* Over the next two months, there were long phone conversations and hand-written love letters. In June, when Norris visited him at his home in Brooklyn Heights, Norman said, "Don't go home. Stay." Even though she was raised in a conservative family, she didn't question her response for a minute. She picked up her three-year-old son and moved to New York.

Norris was daunted neither by Norman's complicated personal life nor his turbu-lent past. "I wasn't intimidated. He always made me feel very secure," she says. When Norman and Norris fell in love, he was still married to his fourth wife, Beverly Bentley, from whom he had been separated for six years. His most recent relation-ship, with Carol Stevens, with whom he had lived during that period and had a daughter, was not faring well.

"Any man who marries six times has to be an optimist," Norris likes to say of his past relationships.

Although there was never a specific moment when Norman said, "Will you marry me?" the couple talked often about marriage. Then in 1977, Norris became pregnant. "We wanted to get married and do the whole thing right. It was definitely a given," she explains.

Securing a divorce from Beverly took another three years. Then, in order to legit-imize his child with Carol, Norman set about arranging one of the swiftest unions and divorces in recorded history. In November 1980 he pulled it off – marrying Carol on a Friday and divorcing her on Saturday in order to marry Norris on Tuesday, November 11.

"It was Veterans Day. Appropriate, I thought," quips Norris. "I confess, at first it gave me a bit of a start, but then I realized it was the right thing to do. And the only thing to do."

Norris and Norman's own wedding was a hastily planned affair, since they weren't sure until Monday that the divorce from Carol had come through. They ran to Tiffany to buy gold wedding bands while friends took care of getting the champagne, a wedding cake, even Norris' champagne-colored satin suit.

The couple was married at home with the children in attendance, including their son, John Buffalo, age two and a half. After the reception, the couple boarded a plane to London, where Norman filmed his cameo role as Stanford White in Milos Forman's movie *Ragtime,* with his new bride, Norris, sitting by his side, playing Stanford White's girlfriend.

Lisa Halaby and

His Majesty King Hussein I of Jordan

Married June 15, 1978

There was always something different about Lisa Halaby. Tall and athletic, she was as beautiful as she was bright. Her friends always knew that this golden girl was destined to lead an exceptional life. Yet even though as an Arab-American she felt a deep connection to her roots, there was no way to predict that she would be transformed into Queen Noor al Hussein, or the "Light of Hussein," the Arabic name chosen for her by Jordan's King Hussein I, a descendant of the prophet Mohammed.

Even she was taken off guard by the swiftness of events that changed her life so radically. "I was literally swept off my feet," says Noor.

The path that led her to a royal romance in the ancient city of Amman began at a time when modern American women were just beginning to assume positions of importance in the work force. She was the daughter of Najeeb Halaby, a first-generation Arab-American who put a high priority on education and spent many years as a dedicated public servant – he was Federal Aviation Administrator – and as president of Pan American World Airways. Lisa attended the best schools and was accepted into Princeton's first co-ed class of '73, where she majored in architecture and urban planning. "She was more determined than most of the females at Princeton," a classmate once observed.

Lisa chose an adventurous career route, heading to Australia to work for an architectural firm with projects in the Middle East. In 1975, she accepted a job with a British urban planning firm in Iran and worked on a large urban development project in Teheran. During that period, she also traveled through Jordan and met Hussein in December 1976, at an official ceremony celebrating the arrival of the national airline's first jumbo jet. The King was then married to Alia Toukan, a Jordanian diplomat's daughter.

Hussein was a teenager standing at the side of his grandfather, King Abdullah, when the king was assassinated. A bullet was also headed for Hussein, but a medal given to him by his grandfather deflected its path. Two years later, in 1953, Hussein, eighteen, succeeded his father, King Talal, to the throne.

As the head of the small Arab state, precariously lodged between Syria, Iraq, Israel and Saudi Arabia, Hussein had many political issues weighing heavily on his mind. When Queen Alia died in a helicopter crash in February 1977, he had to contend with the loneliness of being a single parent to his children, including one child from his first marriage, four from his second marriage, and two with Queen Alia, as well as their adopted daughter.

That same year, Lisa Halaby moved to Jordan to work on a master plan for a pan-Arab Air University in Amman, and later for the national Jordanian airline. She explains: "I often met King Hussein in the course of my work. As director of planning and design projects, I was involved with supervising facilities at the airport, and he, with his love of aviation and his interest in promoting the national airline, would often visit the airport to keep an eye on developments there. It was aviation, a passion that is also shared by my family, which brought us together."

One day, Hussein asked Lisa if she would come to see the newly and poorly built Hashemiyah Palace and advise him on making the necessary repairs. She said she wasn't qualified to assume that kind of responsibility but suggested that he seek the professional advice of top construction firms. Nonetheless, their mutual admiration grew into something more.

Over the course of six weeks, Hussein invited Lisa for lunches that lasted for hours. To escape by themselves, they rode off on motorcycles, even though they were always followed by security guards. They flew in Hussein's helicopter to Aqaba, a port town surrounded by mountains on the northern tip of the Red Sea, where he has a summer home.

Lisa was unprepared for the King's marriage proposal. "While I had very strong feelings and a deep respect for him, a *royal* proposal was not what I had dreamt of as a young girl," Noor recalls today.

The future queen pondered a great deal before giving him an answer, because she wanted to be certain that she was the wife he needed. In the meantime, Hussein wanted to ask her parents for permission for their daughter's hand in marriage, which is customary in Jordan. He had been waiting to visit the United States to ask them in person, but his visit was postponed for political reasons. "Finally, he decided to ask them by telephone, in as traditional manner as possible," says Noor. "Although my parents had known, liked and admired the King for a long time, they were concerned for me and worried about the complexities of royal life and the possible intrigues of a royal court."

At the end of their working days, Hussein invited her to the palace for dinner and sometimes to watch a movie. As Noor remembers, "During that time, we spoke not only of our love and feelings for each other, but also of our future partnership in search for peace in the Middle East and for the benefit of our large Jordanian family. In the end, encouraged by his trust in me, my feelings for him prevailed over my apprehensions."

The public announcement of their engagement took place in May 1978, and plans were set in motion for a wedding to take place the next month. After the engagement, the Washington, D.C.-born Lisa became a Muslim and adopted her new name.

On June 15 at Zahran Palace, the home of Hussein's mother, Queen Zain, the twenty-six-year-old bride – wearing a Dior gown and a diamond solitaire ring given to her as a wedding present – and groom, forty-two, said their vows in Arabic after the Chief Justice of the Islamic Court read from the Koran. The couple shook hands. Although her father was present, neither Noor's mother nor sister were witnesses to the private ceremony, which traditionally excludes women. This was followed by a romantic reception in the palace garden where a seven-layer English fruit cake towered above the five hundred wedding guests, each of whom received a sterling silver box as a memento.

Afterwards, Noor fondly recalls, "We spent the rest of the day together, unencumbered by state affairs, then disappeared off to Aqaba." The couple has two sons and two daughters.

Mary Tyler Moore and S. Robert Levine

Married November 23, 1983

In the early 1980s, for the first time in her life, Mary Tyler Moore was like Mary Richards, her well-known alter ego from the television phenomenon, *The Mary Tyler Moore Show*. To millions of viewers, Mary Richards symbolized the self-reliant '70s woman. She maintained a career and a full life without benefit of a mate. Now the actress, divorced from her second husband, Grant Tinker, who produced the sitcom for the couple's MTM Productions, found herself in the same position. She had moved from Los Angeles to New York and was living on her own.

"I never expected that I would even become seriously involved with anyone, much less marry, and I didn't expect that he'd be Jewish and several years younger than I, either," says Mary.

She had bought an apartment overlooking Central Park – "a little larger than the apartment Mary Richards had" – and spent a year decorating it. She imagined living there for a long time, alone. Married right out of high school, Mary had her first and only child, Richard, when she was nineteen. There were only six months between her two marriages. She had been a wife for her entire adult life.

"This was the first time on my own, experiencing in my early forties what most women experience at a much younger age," she explains. That included dating a lot of different men. "I was loving it, terrified half the time, but because of my delight in the unknown and my love of challenges, I was very happy."

In the fall of 1982, Mary and her parents traveled to Europe. The highlight for her devoutly Catholic parents was an audience with Pope John Paul II. The excitement may have been too much for Mary's mother, Marjorie Moore, who had recovered from a stroke a year before and now developed a serious bronchial infection. The family cut short the trip and arrived back at Mary's apartment in New York, where

Mary immediately phoned her doctor. However, it was Yom Kippur, the Jewish Day of Atonement, and the doctor's service reported that he was in temple.

Another doctor who was covering for him called and advised Mary to bring her mother to the hospital right away. When they arrived at Mount Sinai Hospital's emergency room, the doctor was waiting. "There standing before me in a perfect spotlight," she remembers with cinematic recall, "was S. Robert Levine, M.D., come to your rescue. He was tall, thin and handsome, and he was very gentle, tender and deferential. I watched him as he spent the next hour and a half with my mom being so careful and kind. I thought to myself, 'I really want to get to know this man.' "

Even though the presence of the well-known actress created quite a stir in the emergency room, Robert, a fellow in cardiology and director of Mount Sinai Hospital's Cardiac Rehab Program, was completely focused. "I was preoccupied caring for another doctor's patient," he says. Indeed, notables frequently passed through the hospital, and doctors learned to maintain a respectful distance. Though Robert recognized Mary, he was in college and medical school when *The Mary Tyler Moore Show* was on the air and had pretty much missed the entire seven-year run. A week later, while Mary's mother was recovering at her apartment, Robert visited her and offered Mary his home phone number in case of emergency.

Newly in her "aggressive mode of taking charge and making my own decisions," Mary said to Robert: "Does extreme loneliness come under the heading of emergency?"

"I can't think of a better reason to be awakened in the middle of the night," replied Robert.

The night, after Mary's parents left for their home in Los Angeles, Mary summoned her nerve to call Robert. It was three o'clock in the morning.

"Hi, it's Mary."

"Hi," said Robert.

"Do you cook?" she asked.

"No."

"Well, neither do I," she said. "So I guess we'll have to go out to dinner, won't we?"

On October 1, their first date, dinner at Cafe des Artistes, Mary and Robert felt an immediate bond. Besides being unlike everyone she knew in Hollywood, Robert had a "nobility about himself and a clarity about what his goals were that shone through, and I wanted to be around him," says Mary.

Robert, twenty-nine, who grew up in Brooklyn and Queens, hadn't had the time or energy for a meaningful relationship since he had graduated *summa cum laude* from Loyola-Stritch Medical School in Chicago and begun his specialty training. Now he was talking to a beautiful woman who possessed the qualities he was looking for. "She was very literate, independent, accomplished and had a life of her own," he says. These were the things, he believed, "that make a relationship last."

Still, because of the difference in their ages, Mary's fame and their different faiths,

Mary assumed she was about to enter "one of those wonderful affairs from which both people emerged at some point sadder but wiser and richer for the experience."

Instead, they fell in love. They saw each other two or three times a week when Robert had free time, going to dinner, movies and, because of Mary's love of dance, ballets. Within a few months, Robert moved into Mary's apartment.

One evening, Mary woke up in the middle of the night craving a tuna fish sandwich. For her it was an epiphany when Robert volunteered to go into the kitchen and whip one together. "I had never had anybody do anything so spontaneously loving," she says. "The relationship just felt so natural and right."

So right, in fact, that neither felt the necessity to discuss the obvious strikes against them. From an emotional standpoint, "Robert is a much older person than I am," says Mary. He was also clearly devoted to her. They never brought up marriage but believed nevertheless that the relationship was a permanent one.

In April, they traveled to Israel. Mary, a non-practicing Catholic, wanted exposure to the religion and culture of Robert, his family and his friends. At the Wailing Wall in Jerusalem, Mary had a revelation. Suddenly able to see her life in a clearer light, she knew she wanted to formalize their relationship.

Robert agreed. Back in their room at the King David Hotel, overlooking the wall, they wondered what was stopping them. Robert's brother Michael had just announced his own marriage plans. "We asked ourselves what was different about us and our lives that made us resistant to getting married?" explains Robert.

"It's hard to break those traditional patterns that you either establish for yourself or you are aware of," says Mary.

Their decision to marry, he says, was based on "a conspiracy of events – of being in Israel, of the Wall experience, of my brother announcing that he was getting married."

On November 23, 1983, the night before Thanksgiving, Mary and Robert were married by a rabbi with both of their parents standing at their sides at the Pierre Hotel in New York. Mary, in a mid-calf Victorian dress, and Robert, in a gray three-piece suit, exchanged vows in Hebrew. Each slipped a plain gold wedding band on the other's finger.

Half of the guests were Jewish and half were "all WASP," says Mary. Nevertheless, both halves merged, reveling late into the night and dancing the traditional Israeli *hora*. Atop the wedding cake were two turkeys – one wearing a stethoscope and one wearing ballet shoes.

The party went on so late that the couple missed their early morning plane to an island resort in the Caribbean. Instead, Mary and Robert flew to the Boca Raton Beach Club in Boca Raton, Florida, for a three-day honeymoon before Robert reported back to the hospital.

Shortly after celebrating their tenth anniversary, Mary reflected on all the doubters and cynics with a triumphant smile. "When we got married, they said it wouldn't last, and in our case they really meant it."

Maria Shriver and Arnold Schwarzenegger

Married April 26, 1986

They met in 1977, before the term "power couple" was coined. But if ever there was a couple with power, it is broadcast journalist Maria Shriver and international film star Arnold Schwarzenegger.

At twenty-one, Maria had recently graduated from Georgetown University. She already had a clear direction in which she wanted to take her life – a career in news reporting – and was enrolled in the Westinghouse broadcast-training program. Part of the large, close-knit Kennedy family, Maria had joined the clan at the Robert F. Kennedy Pro-Celebrity Tennis Tournament in Forest Hills, New York, held annually in honor of her late uncle.

Maria's brother, Bobby, had invited Arnold, thirty, to compete though he wasn't a tennis player. The Austrian native was a bodybuilder whose Mr. Olympia competition was the subject of the critically acclaimed 1977 documentary film, *Pumping Iron*. Arnold had become a contender for Hollywood-hero status when he made his acting debut in *Stay Hungry* (1976).

Maria had been introduced to Arnold by news anchor Tom Brokaw at a party the night before the tournament, but it wasn't until she saw him on the court that she truly took notice. Arnold and former football star Rosie Grier were hopelessly losing a doubles game to a pair of ten-year-olds when they removed their shirts and vamped for the crowd.

"Your daughter has a great body," Arnold told Maria's mother, Eunice Kennedy Shriver, that day. He's funny, Maria thought. And gutsy.

Everyone around them sensed the instant chemistry.

That afternoon, Maria impulsively invited Arnold to join her family at their house near the Kennedys' legendary compound in Hyannis Port, Massachusetts. As her brother remarked, "Maria had never met a guy and brought him to the Cape *that* fast."

Eunice, who started the Special Olympics, and Sargent Shriver, the first Peace Corps director and former ambassador to France, were extremely protective of Maria when she was growing up. They kept an eye on whom she dated and made sure of her whereabouts. Before she met Arnold, she had only two other serious boyfriends. Though Arnold was altogether unlike any of Maria's other beaux, he was funny and natural and immediately impressed Maria's parents.

"I was pretty sure when I met him that I would marry him," said Maria. "I admired his independence, his focus, his drive, his humor. I thought I would have a challenging life with him. Not an easy life, but an interesting one."

Arnold saw Maria as someone who could be an equal partner. "It's a big advantage to be with someone who is smart," he explained. "She's not afraid to express her opinion, even though it's not always what I want to hear. I have enough people around me who are yes-people. That's the last thing I need in a wife."

The couple began dating as Maria was working her way up the TV-news ladder, first as a segment producer and eventually as an on-camera reporter. Her big break was a reporting slot for CBS News. Maria wanted to develop her own identity, professionally and personally, before she married. She had set a goal of becoming a network anchor by age thirty. In no hurry to settle down, she would think about marriage then, too. After all, her mother was over thirty when she married. Maria idolized Eunice and had always wanted a marriage as strong and lasting as that of her parents. In 1985, a year ahead of schedule, Maria won the anchor assignment on the *CBS Morning News.*

Arnold was equally determined to succeed. In 1982, he starred in *Conan the Barbarian,* an enormous success, followed by a sequel, *Conan the Destroyer.* Two years later, his phenomenally popular film *The Terminator* thrust him into the role of superstar.

Arnold became an American citizen in 1983, and soon after gained recognition and respect for the active role he took on behalf of the Republican party. Maria, the niece of President John F. Kennedy, was a liberal Democrat. They learned to accept each other's political positions. "The thing people don't understand is that he grew up in a socialist country," says Maria. In America, she adds, "it's natural for immigrants to come wanting government out of their lives. That's why so many become Republicans."

In the summer of 1985, Arnold took Maria home with him to Thal, Austria. While they were in a row boat on the lake where Arnold swam as a child, he asked her to be his wife.

"Are you serious?" asked Maria.

Arnold presented her with a diamond engagement ring. He was serious. "We'd been together eight years, so naturally I said, 'Yes!,' " recalled Maria.

The following spring, the couple's friends and families gathered at the family compound in Hyannis Port for the nuptials. The day before the wedding, Maria's cousin and maid of honor Caroline Kennedy (who would marry Edwin Schlossberg three months later) hosted a luncheon at her mother Jacqueline Onassis' cottage. Thirty guests were served New England clam chowder and kept the soup mugs, which were inscribed *"Maria and Arnold, April 25, 1986, Chowderheads."*

That evening, Arnold's mother, Aurelia, hosted the Austrian-style rehearsal dinner – serving everything from *Wiener schnitzel* to *Sacher torte* – at the Hyannis Port Country Club. Arnold dressed in traditional Tyrolean *lederhosen*. After performing in a skit ("Old MacArnold Had a Farm," sung to the tune of "Old MacDonald", Caroline presented the bridesmaids' gift to Maria – a sterling silver comb, brush, mirror and tray engraved with the bridesmaids' names. Maria, in return, presented the bridesmaids with black lacquer boxes hand painted with images of her grandmother Rose Kennedy's house, where the reception took place.

When Arnold gave his future in-laws a silk-screened photo of Maria made by pop artist Andy Warhol, one of the wedding guests, he told them, "I'm not really taking her away, because I am giving this to you so you will always have her."

"I love her and I will always take care of her. Nobody should worry," Arnold assured the guests.

The next day, April 26, all air traffic within a two-mile radius of the Kennedy compound was forbidden to cruise below two thousand feet. At 11 a.m. Maria, thirty, and Arnold, thirty-eight, entered St. Francis Xavier Church. Arnold wore tails and Maria wore a pearl-edged white satin-and-lace gown, with an eleven-foot train, designed by Marc Bohan of Christian Dior. She carried a bouquet of French posies and roses.

Among the nine bridesmaids, dressed in silk moire in varying shades of blue, pink and violet, were Maria's cousins and Alexa Halaby, younger sister of Queen Noor of Jordan. Former Mr. Universe Franco Columbu was best man. At the ceremony, Oprah Winfrey read Elizabeth Barrett Browning's "How Do I Love Thee?" The couple exited the church to the music of Rodgers and Hammerstein's "The Bridal March."

A champagne lunch reception for four hundred fifty guests began with oysters, cold lobster and chicken breasts and culminated with a seven-foot, eight-tier, carrot-and-pound wedding cake, a replica of the one served when Maria's parents were wed. Peter Duchin's seven-piece band provided music. Since Maria had broken two toes a few days before the wedding, she had to slip on sneakers to dance.

For several years Maria commuted from her home in Los Angeles to New York and Washington, D.C., for her anchor job on NBC's *Sunday Today* and *Weekend Nightly News*. Later Maria started a series of popular prime-time specials that afforded the devoted mother the time to raise her daughter, Katherine Eunice, born in 1989. Another daughter, Christina Aurelia, was born in 1991, followed two years later by a son, Patrick Arnold.

Diane Lander and Neil Simon

Married January 13, 1987

Sure, there's a spunky, good-looking heroine with an adorable daughter and a third act guaranteed to leave audiences with a warm feeling. But this is one romantic comedy Neil Simon will never write.

The first meeting, in November 1986, was in the cosmetics department of Neiman-Marcus in Beverly Hills. Diane Lander, an actress, was modeling and passing out perfume samples when she noticed an interesting man looking at her. He smiled at her. She smiled at him, and then he left the store.

The divorced playwright was about to hand his claim ticket to a parking attendant when he had second thoughts. "If I give him this ticket, I'll never see her again in my life," he told himself. He left his car and returned to the cosmetics department to meet the attractive blonde emanating earthy warmth and pushing Anne Klein perfume.

Neil awkwardly tried to engage her in conversation. He was looking for some perfume, he began. She wanted to know if he had anything special in mind.

After a few minutes of this, Neil blurted out, "Can I see your hand?"

"Can I see yours?" Diane shot back. Judging by his horn-rim glasses, saddle shoes and leather jacket, she assumed he was some kind of intellectual, perhaps a UCLA professor. "What are we doing?" she asked.

"I want to know if you're married," he said.

She wasn't, she said, but flatly refused his invitation for lunch or dinner, since dating customers was prohibited at Neiman-Marcus. She also refused him her phone number.

He didn't give up. He continued chatting, mentioning that he was shopping for a present for his ex-girlfriend's daughter. Diane liked that.

But when he introduced himself, her spirits dropped.

She had dated celebrities before and considered them trouble. At thirty-four, the last thing she wanted in her life was a madcap adventure. She was looking for a solid relationship that would give her security. Her daughter, Bryn, had been conceived during a liaison two years earlier. As a Catholic, Diane decided to raise her on her own.

"I'm not leaving the counter without your number," Neil said, after standing by her side for an hour and a half.

Borrowing her supervisor's pen, Diane jotted down her number. "Inside, in my head, I said, 'Yippee,' " Neil recalls. He didn't find out until later that the connection cost Diane her job.

On their first date, dinner at Morton's, Neil gave her a copy of his play *Biloxi Blues.* "I thought, maybe she won't believe that I'm a playwright," he says. He inscribed it: "I've been waiting to meet you all my life." The madcap adventure was about to begin.

Neil found other ways to get a girl to fall in love with him. The night before Thanksgiving, he kept her company while she baked pies. Then he pulled his lonely guy act and wangled an invitation for Thanksgiving dinner. "When I think back about it, of course he must have been invited to ten different places," she muses.

The next time he came to dinner, Bryn made an appearance. "I didn't know she had a baby," says Neil. "She was the cutest thing I'd ever seen. Diane made dinner, and the baby sat with us in her little high chair and never said a word. Diane put her to bed, and while we were in the living room talking, she kept sneaking out, peering around the corner. Finally, she came in and sat on my lap. I said, 'Uh-oh – I'm caught.' The child was irresistible."

Soon after, on a whim, Diane showed up at Neil's house with a gardener and a truckload of flowers. She surprised him by blanketing his estate with color. "It was so sad," she says. "He had this beautiful house and not a flower at the place."

Neil had met plenty of actresses, but none quite like Diane. She was funny, impetuous, a straight talker and totally unlike so many of the women who were chasing his name and his money. "You feel her presence right away – she almost always brings a cheerful note," says Neil. "And she really is very attuned to the ground, to the earth, everything. She kept telling me to go out and look at the flowers."

True to her Jeffersonville, Indiana, rearing, Diane was impervious to pretense. Although she worked regularly in television – including a stint as Sally, the nurse on *House Calls* – and in commercials, she hated the Hollywood party scene as much as she hated dressing up. "He was getting honored all the time, and every time we turned around, he was putting on a tuxedo," she sighs.

When Neil wanted to take her shopping for fancy clothes on Rodeo Drive, she was miserable. "She doesn't like to wear anything she can't wear on a tractor," he sympathized with a saleswoman.

Neil's past was no secret. He had written about the death of his first wife, Joan, and his difficulties reembarking on romance during his relationship, and eventual marriage, with actress Marsha Mason in the play *Chapter Two.* In fact, in the movie version, Mason virtually played herself. By 1982, he and Marsha had separated. Although he had no desire to remarry at the age of fifty-nine, with two grown daughters, he had launched himself back in the dating world again.

While Diane didn't think she fit into Neil's well-ordered world, she couldn't help falling in love. "He's terribly bright and funny, and when he talks to you, it's like you're the only person on earth," she says.

After a few months, Neil started campaigning for her to move into his house. Diane demurred. She felt she had to be cautious. "I saw it as a wonderful affair," and a passionate one at that, she says. "But I didn't see a future for us. I think he was very distrustful from the divorce from Marsha and I think he was still mourning Joan."

After a month's vacation together in the Hamptons, Neil was determined that Diane move in with him. She continued to resist because she just felt their worlds were too far apart, and they broke up. They got together again in the fall when Diane and Bryn stayed with him in New York during previews for his newest play, *Broadway Bound.*

A turning point for Neil occurred one morning over breakfast. Bryn looked at Neil and asked: "Do you want to be my daddy?"

"Yes, I do," Neil said.

Bryn was quiet for a few moments and said, "Not yet."

"I thought that was astounding," he says. "She sensed you had to bond first."

Diane spent Christmas in Indiana, but just before New Year's, when they both were back in Los Angeles, he again pressed her to live with him.

"I won't do it," she said.

"Well, okay, let's get married," he said.

They were married in a civil ceremony on January 13, 1987, once a most unusual prenuptial agreement was signed. "In principle, I didn't like having a prenuptial, but I understood his position, marrying an actress with a baby, and I went along with it," she says. "But I did say, for all his forty pages, my one stipulation is: I don't want him to write about me or my daughter in my lifetime. I didn't want him observing the relationship so that he could write about it. I wanted him to live it. There were other people in the world he could write about."

The problems started when they bought a beach house in Malibu. The stress of remodeling added to Diane's discomfort in trying to fit into Neil's life. She felt that his advisors and staff, unaccustomed to a woman and child in the picture, came between them. Neither Neil nor Diane was happy.

When the house was completed a year and a half later, the couple split up. Their divorce was amicable, and Neil stayed close to Bryn. "I'd drop her off at his house and sit at the Bel-Air Gate and cry for two hours," says Diane.

"Diane and I would be face to face in the driveway and I could see tears in her eyes, and I thought: What can I do?" says Neil. "I can't say, 'Let's get together again.' By then I thought it was never going to happen. But the frequency of seeing Bryn brought us closer together."

In May 1989, Diane's mother was diagnosed with cancer, and Neil flew to Indiana to see her and Diane. The couple soon started to date again. One night he picked up Diane for a casual dinner, and when they got inside his car, he handed her a small blue box.

"You can either have this or twelve clocks from Tiffany," he quipped.

Inside was an emerald-cut diamond ring, something Diane had told Neil she always wanted.

"Are you asking me to marry you?" asked Diane.

"Yes."

"Well, say it."

"Will you marry me?"

"Yes."

The wedding took place February 10, 1990, at Neil's house, followed by a reception at The Bistro in Beverly Hills. Diane wore an ivory mid-calf skirt, top and circle coat that was a copy of an ensemble designed by the renowned American designer Mainbocher. She chose it from one of Bryn's paper-doll outfits. Neil wore a blue suit he purchased at Neiman-Marcus.

*Diamond engagement rings became popular among the wealthy
in the fifteenth century and have since become a symbol of the groom's good intentions.
"The solitaire diamond, as large and perfect as he could afford, has
for many years been the standard engagement ring," according to a publication on the
subject, London, 1828. Today, seventy-five percent of new brides receive one.*

Florence Griffith and Al Joyner

Married   October   10,   1987

The first time Al Joyner saw Florence Griffith was in a photograph in *Track and Field* magazine in 1978. She was a track star from Los Angeles' Jordan High School. "Wow," the teenager said to himself. "This person runs track?" An equally accomplished track athlete from East St. Louis Lincoln Senior High School, Al couldn't get over how pretty Florence was. "Her facial expression stuck in my mind."

"When I saw her in person, she was even more beautiful," Al recalls. That fateful event occurred two years later at the U.S. Olympic trials in Eugene, Oregon. Neither of them made the U.S. team – though Al qualified in the 110-meter high hurdle race and Florence for the 100- and 200-meter races – but at least Al got to see Florence in the flesh.

During registration, Al, twenty, walked in and spotted the long-haired (and long-nailed) beauty. At first he thought she must be a trainer, because he had never seen such a beautiful athlete, but then he discovered she was the woman in the magazine. Florence, also twenty, didn't even glance at Al. That didn't stop him from deciding at that moment that he was going to marry her.

Florence was standing with a group of women, and Al ambled over to her. "Hello," he said anxiously. "My name is Al Joyner and I'm from East St. Louis, Illinois." He went on to mention where he trained – Arkansas State University – and the event he was competing in. "I thought he was a very nice person," says Florence, but Al was too shy to ask for a date.

When he learned that Florence was training at the University of California at Los Angeles, where his younger sister, Jackie, also a runner, was enrolled, he thought he had it made. "I kept telling Jackie to tell Florence that she had a brother who was crazy about her," says Al. Jackie, however, refused to play Cupid. "She thought I was a kid. She said Florence would never like me."

Al carried Florence's picture in his wallet. Back home he had so many pictures of her on his walls that his friends at college were convinced that they were going together.

The couple saw one another over the next few years at track meets and always said hello and engaged in brief conversations. Al never summoned the nerve to display overt interest. He sent her Christmas cards and phoned her once or twice, but the subject was always something to do with track.

"He never said, 'I would like to date you,' " Florence remembers. "It was just very casual. He was quiet, a very nice young man whom I was curious to find more about because he seemed very respectful of women. I really loved that quality in him because, outside of Al, I didn't know many men who respected women the way I wanted a man to. I was curious whether he was actually like that or if he was putting up a front."

It wasn't a front. Al had three sisters and a strong role model in his mother. "Florence was the woman I think my mother, who passed away in 1981, would have adored. I'd see her at track meets: she's a very beautiful person but she was a great competitor with great sportsmanship qualities. She studied the Bible, she always had a focus and meaning about everything she did. I loved that too. I knew the person I wanted to marry would have to have strong values. God forbid if anything ever happened to me, I'd want a strong woman to carry on with the children."

In 1984, Florence won a silver medal in the 200-meter race at the Los Angeles Summer Olympics, while Al won a gold medal in the triple jump. He returned to Arkansas State with another prize – a promise from Florence that if he ever returned to Los Angeles, she would show him the sights.

Two years later, in October 1986, when Al moved west to train at UCLA for the '88 Olympic Games, he left notice with his friends: "The only reason I won't come back to Jonesboro, Arkansas, is if I marry Florence Griffith."

Al was in L.A. now, but he was still too scared to call Florence. When he pulled into his bank parking lot, however, he saw the woman of his dreams getting out of her car wearing a wedding dress. It was Halloween, and Florence had just left her job as a customer service representative at Union Bank, where the employees dressed in costume for the day.

"Will you keep your promise to show me around?" Al asked.

"Sure, call me and let me know when," said Florence.

A few days later, Florence called her trainer, Bob Kersee, who was Al's trainer – and his brother-in-law after Bob and Jackie wed. Florence heard Al's voice in the background and asked to speak with him. To Al, it was like a sign from God. Finally, he summoned the confidence to ask her out for a date.

"I was totally blown off the planet," says Florence.

They went to dinner at the Black Whale in Marina del Rey. Al talked the whole night, trying to tell her everything he could about himself. Every Tuesday after that, he sent her a bouquet of flowers with a sweet message. Once he got ahead of himself, signing the card, "*Your Future Husband ... Just Joking.*"

Seven was Al's lucky number. Florence was the seventh of eleven children. So at practice on Saturday, July 17, 1987, Al asked Florence to have dinner with him that evening. Bob was pushing her hard that day, and she wasn't sure she'd have enough energy for dinner.

Al persisted. "Make it casual," pleaded Florence, who was too tired to think about dressing up.

He arrived at Florence's mother's house in Watts, where she lived, in a chauffeured limousine. "I wonder who's going somewhere," she thought when she saw the car parked outside.

When she got in the limo, Al put a pillow on the floor and got down on his knees.

"I think you're the most beautiful, straightforward woman in the world and I want to ask you, Will you marry me?"

She couldn't speak.

"I was in Wonderland. This dream for me was coming true," says Florence. Al handed her a box wrapped in baby paper. "Thank you," was all she could say when she saw the two-carat round diamond engagement ring. She cried for forty-five minutes.

On Sunday, Florence was still unable to respond. She and Al went to church with her niece, Khalisha, who, like the rest of the family, was rooting for Florence to accept Al's proposal. Always thoughtful of Khalisha, Al took her and Florence to Chuck E. Cheese, a kids' pizza parlor, where the seven-year-old traded in her winning tickets from an arcade game for rubber letters that spelled out, "YES." She handed the letters to her Aunt Florence with a smile.

"Close your eyes and open your hands," Florence told Al, handing him her answer.

Although they planned an elaborate wedding, the couple was overwhelmed by the expense. Florence already had moved into Al's apartment, even though she worried that her strict, old-fashioned father would find out. On October 1, they woke up to the ground shaking. It was the Whittier earthquake. They both considered it a "wake-up call from God." They decided to marry immediately. Joining them in their quick decision was Florence's best friend, Denelle Sykes, and her fiance, Michael Augustine, who agreed to a double wedding in Las Vegas.

The two couples called as many of their relatives as they could and rented two vans to carry them to Las Vegas the following week. They were married before a waterfall at the Las Vegas Wedding Garden on October 10. Florence wore her Halloween costume with silver shoes. Al wore a tuxedo. Afterward, there was a small reception in their room at the American Hotel and dinner at Caesars Palace.

Nine months later, Florence set a world record for the 100-meter dash and became known to the world as "Flojo," the world's fastest woman. At the 1988 Summer Olympics in Seoul, she won three gold medals in the 100-and 200-meter races and the 400-meter relay and a silver medal in the 1600-meter relay. Subsequently, Al became her coach, and she became his coach. They named their daughter Mary, after Al's mother.

Demi Moore and Bruce Willis

Married November 21, 1987

Within a month after their first meeting, Bruce Willis made his marriage intentions clear to Demi Moore. While he didn't exactly come out and propose, he says he "put the information on the table."

"We could get married," he told her offhandedly as they sat in a steam room.

Since she knew he was only half-serious, Demi sidestepped responding to that first comment. "She laughed at me and gave me a kiss," he recalls.

"I was very serious, but I didn't want to appear serious," explains Bruce. Both had recently exited long-term relationships. Demi was undeniably in love with Bruce, but she was hesitant about formalizing their union so quickly. Bruce, on the other hand, had no doubts.

Response or no response, Bruce told Demi he wanted to buy her a diamond ring. She hesitated. "Why don't we just call it a 'friendship ring'?" suggested Bruce. Not about to let him pick one without her, Demi accompanied him to Tiffany & Co. in Beverly Hills where they selected a five-carat, radiant-cut diamond flanked by triangular diamonds.

When they first met at a movie screening at Hollywood's Cinerama Dome on July 21, 1987, Demi Moore knew all about Bruce Willis' reputation as a bad boy. Bruce was the star of the hit television series *Moonlighting*, a witty war of the sexes, and his every boisterous exploit was fodder for the press.

The night of the screening, Bruce, thirty-two, wanted to stay home, but his friend, comedian Ric Ducommon, coerced him into going. Demi, who was there with pals and knew Ric, made friendly small talk.

"I heard you had a good office at Tri-Star," she said to Bruce of their mutual movie studio.

"Yeah, I'm moving," answered Bruce.

"Wow, okay, he's obviously not that friendly," thought Demi. Hardly one of his groupies, the accomplished twenty-four-year-old had already translated a part on T.V.'s *General Hospital* (which she had landed as a teenager) into starring roles in the movies *Blame It on Rio*, *St. Elmo's Fire* and *About Last Night* ...

Bruce remembers being curt because he was preoccupied by the barrage of paparazzi clamoring for his picture. He actually was happy to meet Demi since he had developed a crush on her when he saw her image on a *St. Elmo's Fire* billboard atop Sunset Boulevard.

After the movie, everyone gathered at a popular restaurant, Lucy's El Adobe. It was there that Bruce zeroed in on Demi. He offered to buy her a drink.

"I don't drink," she said. He bought her a Perrier.

"He was completely and overwhelmingly a gentleman," she recalls. "He was so attentive, like I was the only one in the room, and he was nothing like what anyone had written about him." After they finished their drinks, Bruce invited her to see Ric's show at The Improv. Uncomfortable about leaving her friends behind, Demi couldn't decide. Bruce left without her.

Finally, Demi headed to The Improv. Bruce had a chair waiting for her along with a glass of Perrier. After the show, he carried her backpack and escorted her to her car. When he asked for her phone number, Demi repeated it over and over as Bruce tried to remember it. After a few minutes, Demi told Bruce she'd wait while he went back to the club for a pen.

They both drove to their respective homes in Malibu. When Bruce spotted Demi on the Pacific Coast Highway, he stuck his head out the sunroof of his car, took off his hat and waved. Demi was smitten.

Bruce was overcome. "It was just chemical," he said. "It was pheromones – I was breathing in tiny particles of Demi Moore. She was her pretty, charming Demi-Moore self. Something just clicked."

Bruce called first thing the next morning and asked to spend the day with her. That evening they went out with about eight of his buddies. The following day, he called again. Demi told him she would love to see him, but she was going to see her family in Orange County. "Would you like me to go with you?" asked Bruce.

"He seemed to love and embrace everything about and around me," recalls Demi. "I was truly being swept off my feet."

The next night was their first date alone, dinner at Ivy at the Shore in Santa Monica. Bruce wore a yellow cashmere sweater, yellow silk pants and loafers. "I'll remember that always," says Demi.

As for Bruce, he'll never forget how impressed he was when he took Demi jet skiing. On her first time out, she was literally flying sideways. "He loved me from then on," she believes.

The pair was together every day thereafter – going to movies, walking at the beach, talking until dawn. They discovered that they wanted the same things in life.

Both had persevered to get where they were, having set off on their own at young ages to make it in the world. Demi had been in a brief, teenage marriage, and both had difficult childhoods. Most of all, they both wanted families of their own.

By November, Demi was still not responding to Bruce's marriage talk, but they agreed to have a baby. They would start trying that month.

On November 21, they flew to Las Vegas with friends to see a boxing match. While standing at the gambling tables at the Golden Nugget Hotel, Bruce said again, "We *could* get married, you know." She smiled.

"We were with other people and everyone was joking about how we must have been overwhelmed by this romantic boxing match – just seeing those guys pummel each other," Demi remembers, laughing.

About 10:30, Bruce turned to Demi and said, "I could make one phone call to one guy [Steve Wynn, the hotel's owner] and he could get us married by midnight."

"Let me think about it," Demi responded. She disappeared upstairs to their room and nervously fixed her hair and told her friend, "Okay, I'm going to do it." To Demi, the midnight timing was crucial – it was exactly four months after their first meeting at the movie. She joined Bruce downstairs and said, "Why don't you make that call."

It was 11:25 p.m. when they ran off to the Clark County Marriage License Bureau, open twenty-four hours. When they returned to their room, 7-A, with the license, a female minister greeted them. Demi had grabbed flowers from an urn in the hotel's lobby. The couple got down on bended knees and quietly prayed together before the ceremony. They emerged at the top of the suite's staircase, Demi in a long, Victorian-style, eggplant-colored skirt and blouse and Bruce dressed in a suit and T-shirt.

Three weeks later, Victor Kaufman, head of Tri-Star Pictures, tossed a formal wedding as his gift to them. The extravaganza took place on two sound stages at The Burbank Studios. On one stage, Demi, wearing a traditional high-necked wedding gown (revamped by *Moonlighting* costume designer Robert Turturice), and Bruce, in tails, were remarried by the legendary entertainer and minister Little Richard. A gospel choir serenaded them.

Fulfilling her dream of an old-fashioned staircase entrance, Demi descended stairs borrowed from the set of the television series *Designing Women*. Her twelve brides-maids, including actress Ally Sheedy, wore black versions of her Las Vegas wedding ensemble. Among Bruce's dozen ushers was *Moonlighting* creator Glenn Caron. Demi's brother, Morgan Guynes, gave her away. A sit-down dinner for some four hundred fifty guests was held on the second stage, which had been decorated to resemble Los Angeles' old Cocoanut Grove nightclub. Since Bruce was in the middle of filming the action film *Die Hard*, the couple was unable to take a honeymoon.

Demi and Bruce's daughter, Rumer, was conceived on their Las Vegas wedding night and born the following year in August 1988. Another daughter, Scout, was born in 1991. Three years later, a third daughter, Tallulah, joined the family.

Janet Jones and Wayne Gretzky

Married July 16, 1988

Wayne Gretzky's coach and mentor – his father Walter – put a lot of faith in destiny. But if fate played a role in uniting Wayne and Janet Jones, it stumbled several times before getting it right.

Their inauspicious first meeting occurred during the taping of the television show *Dance Fever* in 1981. Wayne, who is considered the greatest hockey player ever, stepped out of his skates to be a celebrity judge, and Janet, who had moved from St. Louis to Los Angeles to work on the show, was one of the professional dancers. If there were any embers burning, neither of them felt the heat. "We were both nineteen," says Janet. "We were young kids and had exciting careers. We were involved in different relationships. Then he went off and I went off."

Occasionally over the next several years, the Edmonton Oilers center and captain would run into Janet, who by then had segued into movies – *The Flamingo Kid*, *American Anthem*, *A Chorus Line*. Each was still involved with another partner, but they enjoyed saying hello to each other. "We were just acquaintance-friends," says Janet. "For some reason, when we saw each other, once at a restaurant in New York, another time at a party, we had a certain chemistry where we could sit and talk. It wasn't any more than that, because we didn't know each other any better."

At a Lakers-Celtics game at the Los Angeles Forum in June 1987, Wayne and Janet encountered each other again. Their respective relationships had just about ended by then. Janet was at the game with her roommate and best friend Linda Buchanen. Wayne was with his buddy, television star Alan Thicke.

"This was the third or fourth time we're saying 'hi' again," recalls Janet. However, this meeting was different. After the game, Wayne asked Janet if she wanted to join him for a beer.

His choice of bars impressed her. She was aware that most celebrities escaped to the Forum's press lounge, as if they were saying, "I'm a star, watch me get in." But Wayne wasn't the type to flaunt his importance. He invited Janet to join him in the more accessible, though private, Forum Club. "It was very sweet on his part," says Janet, adding that, true to his reputation, "he was humble."

Never mind that Wayne had just led the Oilers to their fourth Stanley Cup championship and won the National Hockey League's Most Valuable Player award. "Not knowing hockey that well, I didn't know enough to know what it meant to the world of sports," she admits.

At this point, Alan, being the suave one, interceded for Wayne, the shy one. He suggested that Janet and Linda join them for dinner at La Serre, a posh French restaurant in the San Fernando Valley.

Neither Wayne nor Janet knew where the other stood romantically, so they were cautious. "We had a tremedous time and a great conversation," recalls Wayne, "We were on the same wavelength." They subtly let the other know they were available. But since Janet lived in Los Angeles and Wayne in Edmonton, he "wondered if it would be another three or four years until we'd see each other again." Since they both had planned trips to New York the following week, Wayne suggested they rendezvous there.

After dinner, Alan stepped in once again. He had Wayne's limo driver take him home, then sent the car back to the restaurant so Wayne could escort Janet home alone. Meanwhile, her roommate Linda left in Janet's car.

Wayne walked Janet to her door. She leaned forward, and he kissed her on the cheek. He said he'd call her about dinner in New York.

Four days later, Wayne called.

Not wanting to hurt their exes' feelings, or to let the press in on their romance, the couple began dating secretly. Shuttling between New York, Toronto, Cleveland, Vancouver and Los Angeles, they sometimes traveled with a friend as a shill.

Once they were together, Janet and Wayne never left each other's side. They learned they had everything in common. From an early age, Janet was as addicted to the dance floor as Wayne was to the ice. As kids, both spent all their energy developing their gifts. By the time they were in their early twenties, both had fulfilled their dreams and seen the world. More importantly, they came from large families – Wayne was one of five children, Janet was one of seven. Both were close to their families and wanted children of their own.

About two months after their first date, they appeared in public at a softball tournament in Vancouver. The news about the couple was out, spreading like wildfire.

"It was his soft, sensitive side that turned me on," says Janet. "Because I was a tomboy, I was always attracted to athletic men. You wouldn't think it mixed, the hockey player and the sensitivity, but the combination sparked it for me."

Wayne reflects, "So many men marry women who remind them of their mothers. Janet reminded me so much of my father – how he treats people, his work ethic and the way he praises and constructively criticizes."

In January 1988, Wayne had an engagement ring made for Janet. Years earlier, he had purchased a three-carat round diamond, planning to give it to his future bride. One night, when Janet was shooting a workout video in South Carolina and Wayne was in Edmonton, they were involved in a long-running phone conversation. As it often did, the discussion turned to children, and how both wanted them someday.

"Don't you want to be married when you have children?" Wayne finally asked.

"Absolutely," said Janet.

"Will you marry me?" he asked.

"Yes!" said Janet.

Janet didn't know that Wayne had already called her mother, Jean, for her permission, since Janet's father, Bob, had died when she was seventeen.

A week later, Janet flew to Edmonton. Wayne met her at the airport with the ring.

On July 16, 1988, Janet and Wayne, both twenty-seven, were married before some eight hundred people at St. Joseph's Basilica in Edmonton in what was billed as "Canada's Royal Wedding." Being Mr. Nice Guy, points out Janet, Wayne couldn't say "no" to anyone on the ever-expanding guest list.

Like models for the top of a wedding cake, the groom wore tails and his beautiful bride wore a white gown hand-beaded with thousands of pearls. It was designed by a neighbor of Janet's in Los Angeles. Hockey star Eddie Mio was best man and Janet's sister Jeanette was maid of honor. Following the 5 p.m. ceremony, the couple hosted a sit-down dinner at the Westin Hotel, where Alan Thicke was master of ceremonies. Since both have a weakness for cars, Wayne bought Janet a cream-colored Rolls-Royce Corniche as a wedding present. They consider a pre-wedding trip to Hawaii to be their honeymoon.

One month after the wedding, Number 99 made sports headlines again when he was traded to the Los Angeles Kings. Contrary to popular belief, the transaction was not conceived and orchestrated by Janet. "I might have had something to do with the place he was traded to," she says. Wayne says it was his decision to leave the Oilers. Soon after, their daughter, Paulina, was born. She was followed by sons Ty and Trevor.

Kimberley Conrad and Hugh Hefner

Married July 1, 1989

Throughout the 1960s, '70s and '80s, no one lived the life of a playboy more completely than Hugh Hefner, editor-in-chief of *Playboy* magazine and founder of the Playboy empire.

Hef – as he was known since he was a teenager in Chicago – exuberantly played the field, frequently spending his time with the women who posed for the magazine's famous nude centerfolds. He separated in the early '50s from his wife and college sweetheart, Mildred, the mother of his son, David, and daughter, Christie, the latter who would become chairman and chief executive officer of his company. But Hef fully embraced the free-living philosophy that he had been espousing since founding his magazine in 1953.

"I was absolutely convinced I would never marry again," he says. "I was raised in a traditional Protestant home and believed all the things you wanted to believe back then. But I was married just out of college, and it was not a happy marriage. I'm a very romantic person, but I'd become convinced that marriage and romance, if not polar opposites, were certainly not the same thing."

That was still his attitude at age sixty-one, after four decades of bachelorhood, when Kimberley Conrad, twenty-four, appeared at his Los Angeles estate, Playboy Mansion West, in January 1988. The fashion model from Vancouver came to his sylvan grounds for a Helmut Newton photo session. But it wasn't the first time they had met. She was *Playboy's* featured Playmate that month, and in 1989 would become Playmate of the Year. Hef had met Kimberley six months earlier at another photo session at the Mansion. At the time, he was involved with another Playmate. Now he was unattached, and he invited Kimberley to join him and some friends for an evening screening of a French film. She declined. He invited her to view part two the next night; again, she declined.

But that next night, having completed her photo session, Kimberley decided to join Hef in the dining room after the screening. "I'm really interested in you, and I would like to spend some time with you," Hef told her when he finally had a moment alone with her in the Great Hall.

"I don't really know you," said a wary Kimberley.

"Well, how are you going to get to know me if you don't spend any time with me?" responded Hef. He recalls being aware that Kimberley didn't go out with just anyone, having "seen other guys making pitches at her go down in flames." He wasn't planning on being one of them.

They spent the rest of the evening talking. Once Kimberley knew Hef was sincerely interested in her, she let down her guard. They fell in love in the space of a few hours. The following weekend, she moved in. One week later, her two dogs and a cat joined Hef's menagerie. In two months' time, Hef "knew the unthinkable," he quips today – he wanted to marry her.

What makes the world's most famous bachelor decide to marry for the second time? Why Kimberley? "A very classy lady," he says. "Common interests – love of animals, love of movies, similar sense of humor. And she was the first person I'd met whom I could imagine having children with. She was born in Alabama and is Methodist in background, the same as me.

"Much of *Playboy* and my lifestyle has been a reaction to the repression of my Methodist background," he continues. "But underneath it, I am a very sentimental, very romantic person whose values are really very traditional. It's only the repressive and hurtful parts of Puritanism that I rebelled against. Without knowing it, I was ready to settle down, and I met somebody who for the first time I thought, I'll never meet anyone I care more about."

After about six months, Hef broached the subject of marriage in a general sort of way, to "test the water."

"Don't talk about marriage unless you're serious," Kimberley would tell him.

By July he was serious. One evening, after Kimberley beat Hef and his buddy at a game of foosball, Hef walked her to the wishing well at the front of the house.

"Would you like to marry me?" he asked.

She paused for a moment and said teasingly, "Do I have to answer you right away?"

"Of course not," said Hef, taken aback.

"Of course I will," she said. She reminded him that the last time they stood by the well together was a few weeks earlier when a television reporter asked them each to toss a coin and make a wish.

"This is what I wished for," confessed Kimberley.

"This is what I wished for too," said Hef.

She received an engagement ring with an emerald-cut diamond and they were married a year later, on July 1, 1989. The ceremony took place by the wishing well, followed by a reception for five hundred guests, complete with champagne, caviar, dinner and dancing to a seventeen-piece orchestra. The couple spent their wedding night at the Mansion.

As far as progeny were concerned, Hef clung to part of his Playboy ideology. To prolong their romance, he says, he wanted to postpone having children for a while. But a month after the wedding, Kimberley became pregnant. Their son, Marston, was born on April 9 – his father's birthday. A second son, Cooper, was born the following year. Hef says the romance continues to flourish.

Masako Owada and Crown Prince Naruhito of Japan

Married June 9, 1993

It was destined that Crown Prince Naruhito would be heir to the one hundred twenty-sixth Chrysanthemum Throne, a sixteen-century-old dynasty and the world's oldest monarchy. The mystery was the identity of the woman he would select as his wife and Japan's future empress. The young prince said that finding a wife was a quest comparable to climbing Mount Fuji.

He had been introduced to Masako Owada in October 1986, at a string quartet recital and tea in honor of Princess Elena of Spain at a palace near the imperial grounds. It was an arranged meeting, or *o-miai*, devised by Kensuke Yanagiya, a force in the Foreign Ministry who had known Masako since she was a child. Masako's name was a last-minute addition to the list of forty girls invited for Naruhito's inspection.

Although she graduated *magna cum laude* in Harvard's class of 1985, is fluent in three languages and had earned a reputation as a tough trade negotiator with Japan's Ministry of Foreign Affairs, Masako must have been the dark horse. She was a commoner and a brainy, successful, modern woman, used to traveling alone, even wearing sexy bathing suits in Hawaii. Her independence and fast-track career broke with all historical precedent for the submissive royal wife who would have to walk several paces behind her husband and promptly produce an heir.

While her father, Hisashi Owada, became Japan's Vice Minister of Foreign Affairs in 1991, her family was not at the top of the royals' A-list. There was a hint of scandal in the history of her grandfather's company: under a prior executive, it had been cited for deadly chemical dumping in what became Japan's most infamous industrial pollution catastrophe.

But Naruhito immediately formed a "strong and good" impression of the pretty girl who had worn a blue dress to the recital and who had just passed her foreign ministry exam. A few chaperoned dates occurred in April 1987. Third parties let

Masako know that Naruhito was interested in getting closer. She was unenthusiastic. He wasn't her type, she informed the go-betweens.

The eldest son of Emperor Akihito and grandson of Hirohito was hardly experienced in the ways of women. It was believed that he never had given his heart to anyone and no one took it away. Instead, he spent his time deep in the contemplation of medieval water transport, one of his favorite subjects. He also enjoyed mountain climbing, fine wine and playing the viola and violin.

A year later, Masako left for Oxford for two years, and Naruhito's official search committee, the Imperial Household Agency, failed to turned up another marriage candidate as appealing to the prince as Masako. The checklist included purity (the woman had to be a virgin), size (shorter than the five-foot-five prince), age (early twenties) and religion (either Shinto or Buddhist — Akihito is the spiritual head of Shinto). Many contenders reportedly leapt into marriages in order to remove themselves from the possibility of entering into a life cloistered behind the royal moat in Tokyo's Imperial Palace.

"I'm probably going to challenge Prince Charles for the gold medal in marrying late," he moaned on his thirty-second birthday.

Five years after their first meeting, an intermediary, possibly Yanagiya, made overtures to Masako to resume the courtship, even though Masako now had another strike against her — she was pushing thirty. A meeting was arranged. Then on October 3, 1992, at an imperial duck-hunting ground outside Tokyo, Naruhito asked, "Will you marry me?" Masako didn't answer.

The frustrated young man reportedly called for a heart-to-heart with his mother, Empress Michiko. She supposedly decided to take matters into her own hands and devised a meeting with Masako. As the first commoner to marry a future emperor, in 1959, she knew first-hand about the difficulties of adapting to royal life. She endured enormous prejudice from other royals and was believed to have suffered a nervous breakdown and a miscarriage. Because of her own experiences, Empress Michiko could easily understand why Masako was rejecting her son and pledged her personal support and protection.

Masako's meeting with the Empress turned the tide. Two months later, on December 12, the couple met again at Naruhito's palace.

"Will you accept my proposal?" he asked. "You may be apprehensive about becoming a member of the Royal Family. But Masako-san, I will protect you for my entire life."

"If I can be of support to you, I would like to accept humbly. Since I am accepting, I will work hard to make Your Highness happy and also be able to look back on my life and think, 'It was a good life,' " replied Masako.

Masako received a ring mounted with a rare, large domestic pearl, surrounded by diamonds, during a ceremony of exchanging betrothal presents. It is believed she also received a two-and-one-half-carat diamond engagement ring and a dark navy sapphire ring. She resigned from her job and promptly began studying the fine points of palace etiquette, Japanese waka poetry and calligraphy.

The wedding day, June 9, 1993, was declared a national holiday. According to tradition, the Emperor and Empress could not be among the eight hundred and twelve invited guests seated outside the Kashikodokoro shrine on the Imperial Palace grounds. They watched the proceedings on their high-definition television.

The private Shinto ceremony, attended only by the Chief Ritualist and a few attendants, began at precisely ten o'clock in the morning. Naruhito, thirty-three, wearing a kimono and laden with crown and scepter, entered the simple wood shrine containing the spirit of the sun goddess Amaterasu, matriarch of the Royal Family. Seated inside was his twenty-nine-year-old bride, adorned with lacquered hair and dressed in a *juni-hitoe*, a traditional twelve-layer wedding kimono made of colorful silk. The dress weighed thirty pounds and had a price tag of $300,000. Naruhito read a matrimonial pledge. Masako was silent. Instead of exchanging rings and vows, they sipped sacred sake.

That evening, the couple changed into Western clothes for a parade through Tokyo in a Rolls-Royce convertible. Naruhito wore a suit and Masako wore a sleeveless ivory silk gown with petal jacket designed by Japan's leading couturier, Hanae Mori. The fabric was woven with gold into a cloud design, the same pattern that was used in the dress worn by Michiko for her 1959 wedding. Masako's diamond necklace and tiara were gifts from the Empress.

At Naruhito's residence, Togu Palace, the couple was feted at a dinner party. A wooden chest filled with rice cakes was placed in their bedroom. As a fertility rite, it was buried four days later. The couple attended six additional banquets over the next three days. Regarding future offspring, Masako commented that she hoped her husband didn't want "to have enough to form a family orchestra."

Acknowledgments

It sounded so simple – writing about some famous love stories. Ultimately it took dozens of connections to get to the people we needed, including the historians who could help unravel some complex histories.

David Nelson, A. Scott Berg, Toni Howard, Boaty Boatwright, Jerry Weintraub, Robert Dallek, Linda Bruckheimer and Lina Toukan, legal and personal assistant to Her Majesty Queen Noor, went out of their way to assist. Special thanks, also, go to Cri Cri Solak-Eastin, Mari Matsumoto and the Diamond Information Center. Precious links, or the clarification of facts, couldn't have been made without the kindnesses of Paul Bloch, Mary Jane Wick, Senator William Cohen, Richard Rosenzweig, Bill Farley, Jody Horwitz, Pat Kingsley, Heidi Schaeffer, George Goodwin, Mal Hoffs, Charles Silverberg, Roger Richman, Ali Gould, Larry Thompson, Kenji Okuhira, British Consulate vice-consul of information John Houlton, Marc Wanamaker of Bison Archives, Ned Comstock at the University of Southern California Cinema-

Acknowledgments

Television Library, Dr. Peter Loewenberg, Christina Papadopoulos, Heyden Herrera, Robert Cohn, Rik Krulish, Henry Blackham, Kenneth Harris C.B.E., Mr. Lynn Cothren, Jeff Silverman, and thanks go to Andrea Dovichi for her early inspiration.

Also, special thanks to researcher Erin Douglass and for the able assistance of Christy Bray, Kathy McGaw, Rosanne Lodato and Gillian Marcus.

The research librarians at the John F. Kennedy and Lyndon B. Johnson Libraries, as well as the reference librarians at the Academy of Motion Picture Arts and Sciences' Margaret Herrick Library, the Beverly Hills Public Library and the Santa Monica Public Library were all extraordinary.

We owe absolute gratitude to those "legends" who corresponded with us – Michael Douglas, Dale Evans, Coretta Scott King, Sophia Loren and Dolly Parton – and to those who granted interviews: Shakira Caine, Norris Church, Maria Cole, Diandra Douglas, Hugh Hefner, Janet Jones and Wayne Gretzky, Florence and Al Joyner, Diane Lander and Neil Simon, Demi Moore and Bruce Willis, Mary Tyler Moore and S. Robert Levine, Priscilla Presley, Jehan Sadat, Beverly Sills and Peter Greenough, Nancy Reagan and Joanne Woodward.

Our hearts are open to encouraging family members and friends, as well as to utterly understanding *Los Angeles Times* editors Janice Mall, Pamm Higgins and Mary Rourke, who witnessed deadlines pass repeatedly. And we send special valentines to Jacqueline Green of Jacqueline Green Public Relations and Maureen Erbe and Rita A. Sowins of Maureen Erbe Design. Finally, our heartfelt thanks to our "Angels" at the Press – Jean Penn, Scott McAuley, Ellen Hoffs and Paddy Calistro.

— *B.G.K. AND W.H.G.*

Credits

GRATEFUL ACKNOWLEDGMENT IS MADE TO THE FOLLOWING FOR PERMISSION TO REPRINT PREVIOUSLY PUBLISHED MATERIAL:

Sigmund Freud letter, Copyright © 1953 A. W. Freud *et al.*, reprinted by arrangement with Mark Paterson & Associates.

Letters by Scott and Zelda Fitzgerald, from *Zelda,* by Nancy Winston Milford. Copyright © 1971 by Nancy Winston Milford. Reprinted by permission of Harold Ober Associates Incorporated.

Rivera quotations, from *My Art, My Life: An Autiobiography,* by Diego Rivera with Gladys March. Copyright © 1960 by Gladys Stevens March. Reprinted by permission of Carol Publishing Group.

Windsor quotations, from *The Heart Has Its Reasons: The Memoirs of the Duchess of Windsor,* by Wallis Warfield Windsor, Random House, New York. Copyright © 1956 by the Duchess of Windsor.

Lucille Ball and Desi Arnaz quotations, from *A Book,* by Desi Arnaz, William Morrow and Company, Inc., New York, 1976; printed with permission of Desilu, Too.

King quotations, from *My Life with Martin Luther King, Jr.*, (Revised Edition) by Coretta Scott King, Copyright © 1993 by Coretta Scott King. Reprinted by permission of Henry Holt and Company, Inc.

GRATEFUL ACKNOWLEDGMENT IS MADE TO THE FOLLOWING FOR PERMISSION TO PRINT PHOTOGRAPHS USED IN THIS BOOK:

Cover: Joanne Woodward and Paul Newman, in *The Long Hot Summer,* from UPI/Bettmann. Roses, ring by Henry Blackham, Los Angeles.

page ii: Ring photo by Henry Blackham, Los Angeles.

page xi: Rose photo by Henry Blackham, Los Angeles.

page 2: Sigmund and Martha Freud, wedding portrait, A. W. Freud *et al.*, by arrangement with Mark Paterson & Associates.

page 8: Zelda and Scott Fitzgerald photo, taken from Zelda's scrapbook, Papers of F. Scott Fitzgerald. Manuscripts Division. Department of Rare Books and Special Collections, Princeton University Library.

page 14: Frida Kahlo and Diego Rivera, four years after their first wedding, from UPI/Bettmann.

page 18: Claudia Taylor and Lyndon Johnson, honeymoon photo, Lyndon B. Johnson Library.

page 22: Ozzie and Harriet Nelson, wedding portrait, courtesy of David Nelson.

page 26: The Duke and Duchess of Windsor, wedding photo, from UPI/Bettmann.

page 32: Carole Lombard and Clark Gable, wedding photo, courtesy of the Academy of Motion Picture Arts and Sciences.

page 36: Lucille Ball and Desi Arnaz, honeymoon photo, from UPI/Bettmann.

page 40: Dale Evans and Roy Rogers, wedding photo, courtesy of the Rogerses.

page 44: Maria Hawkins and Nat King Cole, wedding photo, courtesy of Maria Cole.

page 48: Jehan Safwat Raouf and Anwar Sadat, wedding photo, courtesy of Jehan Sadat.

Credits

page 52: Nancy Davis and Ronald Reagan, wedding photo, courtesy of the Ronald Reagan Presidential Library.

page 56: Coretta Scott and Martin Luther King, Jr., wedding photo by Alexander Adams, Copyright © Coretta Scott King collection.

page 60: Jacqueline Bouvier and John F. Kennedy, wedding photo, from the John F. Kennedy Library.

page 64: Marilyn Monroe and Joe DiMaggio, wedding photo, from UPI/Bettmann.

page 68: Grace Kelly and His Serene Highness Prince Rainier III of Monaco, wedding photo, courtesy of Bison Archives.

page 74: Beverly Sills and Peter Greenough, wedding photo, courtesy of Library of Congress.

page 78: Joanne Woodward and Paul Newman, wedding photo, courtesy of the Newmans.

page 82: Alma Johnson and Colin Powell, wedding photo, courtesy of the office of General Colin L. Powell, USA (Ret.).

page 86: Sophia Loren and Carlo Ponti, wedding photo by Tazio Secchiaroli, courtesy of the Pontis.

page 90: Dolly Parton and Carl Dean, wedding photo, courtesy of the Deans.

page 94: Priscilla Beaulieu and Elvis Presley, wedding photo, courtesy of Graceland Archives.

page 98: Shakira Baksh and Michael Caine, wedding photo, courtesy of the Caines.

page 102: Hillary Rodham and Bill Clinton, three years after their wedding, Arkansas Democrat-Gazette.

page 106: Diandra and Michael Douglas, photo from the Douglas private collection.

page 110: Norris Church and Norman Mailer, pre-wedding photo by Robert Belott, courtesy of the Mailers.

page 114: Lisa Halaby and His Majesty King Hussein I, engagement announcement photo, courtesy Their Royal Highnesses Queen Noor and King Hussein I.

page 118: Mary Tyler Moore and S. Robert Levine, wedding photo by Fred Marcus, courtesy of the Levines.

page 122: Maria Shriver and Arnold Schwarzenegger, wedding photo, UPI/Bettmann.

page 126: Diane Lander and Neil Simon, wedding photo, by Michael Jacobs.

page 132: Florence Griffith and Al Joyner, wedding photo, courtesy of the Joyners.

page 136: Demi Moore and Bruce Willis, wedding photo by Annie Leibovitz, courtesy of the Willises.

page 140: Janet Jones and Wayne Gretzky, wedding photo, courtesy of the Gretzkys.

page 144: Kimberley Conrad and Hugh Hefner, wedding photo by David Kennerly, courtesy of the Hefners.

page 148: Masako Owada and Crown Prince Naruhito wedding photo courtesy of the Diamond Information Center, Copyright © Kyodo News Service.

page 152: Ring photo by Henry Blackham, Los Angeles.

Bibliography

DESI ARNAZ, *A Book,* William Morrow and Company, Inc., New York, 1976

PENELOPE BALOGH, *Freud: A Biographical Introduction,* Charles Scribner's S New York, 1971

CHARLES BARTLETT (interview), John F. Kennedy Library Oral History Project, 1965

JIM BISHOP, *The Days of Martin Luther King, Jr.,* G.P. Putnam's Sons, New York, 1971

SARAH BRADFORD, *Princess Grace,* Stein and Day Publishers, New York, 1984

MATTHEW J. BRUCCOLI, *The Life of F. Scott Fitzgerald,* Carroll & Graf Publishe Inc., New York, 1993

J. BRYAN III AND CHARLES J.V. MURPHY, *The Windsor Story,* William Morrow and Company, Inc., New York, 1979

JAMES MACGREGOR BURNS, *John Kennedy: A Political Profile,* Harcourt, Brace Company, New York, 1959

MICHAEL CAINE, *What's It All About?,* Turtle Bay Books, New York, 1992

ROBERT A. CARO, *The Years of Lyndon Johnson: The Path to Power,* Alfred A. Knopf, New York, 1982

RONALD WILLIAM CLARK, *Freud: The Man and the Cause,* Random House, Inc., New York, 1980

ED CLAYTON, *Martin Luther King: The Peaceful Warrior,* Prentice-Hall, Inc., New York, 1964

MARIA COLE WITH LOUIE ROBINSON, *Nat King Cole: An Intimate Biography,* William Morrow & Company, Inc., New York, 1971

DAVID CONOVER, *Finding Marilyn: A Romance,* Grosset & Dunlap, New York, 1981

ROBERT DALLEK, *Lone Star Rising: Lyndon Johnson and His Times 1908-196* Oxford University Press, New York, 1991

ANNE EDWARDS, *Early Reagan: The Rise to Power,* William Morrow and Company, Inc., New York, 1987

ANNE EDWARDS, *The Grimaldis of Monaco,* William Morrow and Company, Inc., Nev York, 1992

STEVEN ENGLUND, *Grace of Monaco: An Interpretive Biography,* Doubleday & Company, Inc., Garden City, New York, 1984

PETER GAY, *Freud: A Life for Our Time,* W.W. Norton & Co., New York, 1988

DORIS KEARNS GOODWIN, *The Fitzgeralds and the Kennedys,* Simon and Schuste New York, 1987

LESLIE GOURSE, *Unforgettable: The Life and Mystique of Nat King Cole,* St. Martin's Press, New York, 1991

Bibliography

ADELA GREGORY AND MILO SPERIGLIO, *Crypt 33: The Saga of Marilyn Monroe – The Final Word,* Carol Publishing Group, Secaucus, New Jersey, 1993

FRED LAWRENCE GUILES, *Norma Jean,* McGraw-Hill Book Company, New York, 1969

GORDON LANGLEY HALL AND ANN PICHOT, *Jacqueline Kennedy: A Biography,* Frederick Fell, Inc., New York, 1964

WARREN G. HARRIS, *Gable and Lombard,* Simon and Schuster, New York, 1974

RONALD HAVER, *David O. Selznick's Hollywood,* Alfred A. Knopf, New York, 1980

C. DAVID HAYMAN, *A Woman Named Jackie,* Lyle Stuart, Secaucus, New Jersey, 1989

HEYDEN HERRERA, *Frida: A Biography of Frida Kahlo,* Harper & Row Publishers, New York, 1983

CHARLES HIGHAM, *Lucy: The Life of Lucille Ball,* St. Martin's Press, New York, 1986

A.E. HOTCHNER, *Sophia: Living and Loving Her Own Story,* William Morrow and Company, Inc., New York, 1979

ERNEST JONES, M.D., *The Life and Work of Sigmund Freud,* Basic Books, Inc., New York, 1953

ROGER KAHN, *Joe & Marilyn: A Memory of Love,* William Morrow and Company, Inc., New York, 1986

JOSEPH NATHAN KANE, *Facts About Presidents,* The H. W. Wilson Co., New York, 1989

CORETTA SCOTT KING, *My Life with Martin Luther King, Jr.* (Revised Edition), Henry Holt and Company, Inc., New York, 1993

ANDRE LEVOT, *F. Scott Fitzgerald: A Biography,* Doubleday & Company, Inc., Garden City, New York, 1983

DAVID LEVERING LEWIS, *King: A Biography,* University of Illinois Press, Urbana, 1970

HOWARD MEANS, *Colin Powell: Soldier/Statesman – Statesman/Soldier,* Donald A. Fine, Inc., New York, 1992

JAMES R. MELLOW, *Invented Lives: F. Scott and Zelda Fitzgerald,* Houghton Mifflin Company, Boston, 1984

NANCY MILFORD, *Zelda: A Biography,* Harper & Row Publishers, New York, 1970

ARTHUR MIZENER, *F. Scott Fitzgerald,* Thames and Hudson, New York, 1987

JOE MORELLA, EDWARD Z. EPSTEIN AND ELENA OUMANO, *Paul and Joanne,* Delacorte Press, 1988

OZZIE NELSON, *Ozzie,* Prentice-Hall, Englewood Cliffs, New Jersey, 1973

ELENA OUMANO, *Paul Newman,* St. Martin's Press, New York, 1989

HERBERT S. PARMET, *JFK: The Struggles of John F. Kennedy,* Dial Press, New York, 1980

Bibliography

Priscilla Beaulieu Presley with Sandra Harman, *Elvis and Me,* G.P. Putnam's Sons, New York, 1985

Judy Balaban Quine, *The Bridesmaids: Grace Kelly, Princess of Monaco, and Six Intimate Friends,* Weidenfeld & Nicolson, New York, 1989

Nancy Reagan with William Novak, *My Turn: The Memories of Nancy Reagan,* Random House, New York, 1989

Ronald Reagan, *An American Life,* Simon and Schuster, New York, 1990

William L. Roper, *Roy Rogers, King of the Cowboys,* T. S. Denison & Co., Inc., Minneapolis, 1971

David Roth, *Sacred Honor: Colin Powell, The Inside Account of His Life and Triumphs,* Zondervan Publishing House, Grand Rapids, Michigan, 1993

Charles Samuels, *The King: A Biography of Clark Gable,* Coward-McCann, Inc., New York, 1962

Wendy Sauers, editor, *Elvis Presley: A Complete Reference,* McFarland & Co., Inc., Jefferson, North Carolina, 1984

Beverly Sills, *Bubbles: A Self-Portrait,* The Bobbs-Merrill Company, Inc., Indianapolis, 1976

Beverly Sills and Lawrence Linderman, *Beverly: An Autobiography,* Bantam Books, Inc., New York, 1987

Alfred Steinberg, *Sam Johnson's Boy: A Close-up of the President from Texas,* Macmillan, New York, 1968

Larry Swindell, *Screwball: The Life of Carole Lombard,* William Morrow and Company, New York, 1975

Lyn Tornabene, *Long Live the King: A Biography of Clark Gable,* G. P. Putnam's Sons, New York, 1976

Andrew Turnbull, *Scott Fitzgerald,* Charles Scribner's Sons, New York, 1962

Christopher Warwick, *Abdication,* Sidgwick & Jackson, London, 1986

Jane Ellen Wayne, *Clark Gable: Portrait of a Misfit,* St. Martin's Press, New York, 1993

Jane Ellen Wayne, *Gable's Women,* Prentice-Hall, New York, 1987

Wallis Warfield Windsor, *The Heart Has Its Reasons: the Memoirs of the Duchess of Windsor,* David McKay Company, Inc., New York, 1956

Bertram D. Wolfe, *The Fabulous Life of Diego Rivera,* Stein and Day Publishers, New York, 1963

Index

Index

About the Authors

Wendy Howard Goldberg

"I love you very much. I'd like to spend the rest of my life with you – will you marry me?" Leonard Goldberg, an illustrious motion picture and television producer and longtime bachelor, asked Wendy Howard at the end of an intimate dinner. Her diamond engagement ring came a little later inside a heart-shaped box of chocolates. They were married in Los Angeles in 1972 at a private ceremony followed by dinner at Chasen's. They have a daughter, Amanda.

Goldberg has worked in the public and private sectors. She was appointed to the California Arts Council and founded the California State Summer School for the Arts. She launched the annual Governor's Awards for the Arts program and has chaired numerous fundraisers for various non-profit organizations. In addition, she has worked as a marketing executive for Max Factor and Revlon.

Betty Goodwin

Betty Goodwin received a proposal of marriage from attorney Keith Klevan a few days after the Northridge earthquake of January 1994, while she was writing this book. The couple had been discussing marriage plans, but an act of God moved things forward in a hurry. They were married four months later in a garden ceremony in Los Angeles.

In her professional life, Goodwin covers the social scene for the *Los Angeles Times* where her syndicated column, "Screen Style," on movie and television costumes, also appears. She has covered the entertainment industry, fashion and style for many national publications, including *Harper's Bazaar*, *Vogue*, *TV Guide*, and the *New York Times*. *Marry Me!* follows her other books *Hollywood du Jour: Lost Recipes of Legendary Hollywood Haunts* and *L.A. Inside Out: The Architecture and Interiors of America's Most Colorful City*.

Marry Me!

Maureen Erbe Design

Marry Me! was designed by the award-winning graphic design firm Maureen Erbe Design in Los Angeles. The design was executed while Erbe was planning her wedding to photographer Henry Blackham, whose work appears in *Marry Me!* The Cupid used throughout this book was borrowed from the couple's wedding invitation. Two-year-veteran bride and senior designer at the firm, Rita A. Sowins, married to clothing designer James D. Sowins, advised the newlyweds and kept the project on course. Erbe Design counts numerous corporations and institutions among its clients, and is credited with the design and co-authorsip of *Made in Japan: Transistor Radios of the 1950s and 1960s* (1993).

Marry Me!

Marry Me! was produced on an Apple Macintosh IIci. Programs used include QuarkXPress and Adobe Photoshop. The font used in the body text is Garamond Three 10.5 point; the font used in the chapter heads is Shelly Andante 17 point.